A Guide to Reforming
the U.S. Health Sector

Recovery

Michael F. Cannon

CATO
INSTITUTE

Washington, DC

ISBN 978-1-952223-84-6 (print)
ISBN 978-1-952223-85-3 (digital)

Cover design by Jon Meyers.

Printed in the United States.

Cato Institute
1000 Massachusetts Ave. NW
Washington, DC 20001
www.cato.org

Recovery

re·cov·er·y

noun

- the act or process of getting better; improvement
- the process of getting something back that was lost or almost destroyed

—*Cambridge Dictionary*

Contents

1. INTRODUCTION

When we find a lump, when the results come back positive, or when we trade our clothes for a hospital gown, we are at our most vulnerable.

Modern medicine can make us less so. It manages and even cures illnesses that were once incurable or even a death sentence. The U.S. health sector brings a disproportionate share of these innovations to the world.[1]

But not to everyone. When effective preventive measures and treatments exist, many patients cannot afford them. Even when they can, what patients get is too often of such poor quality that it does more harm than good.

A large part of the reason why so many patients fall through the cracks is their own government.

Government exists to serve the people. In the United States, however, countless state and federal laws block innovations that would improve health care access and quality. Without exception, lawmakers enact these laws in the hope of reducing costs and improving quality. Without exception, they do extraordinary and irreversible harm to patients.

This book explains how state governments prevent medical professionals and entrepreneurs from offering higher-quality, lower-cost care. It explains how Congress denies consumers both control of trillions of dollars of their own earnings and the right to make their own medical decisions. It explains how Congress makes health care increasingly less affordable, jeopardizes patient health by promoting low-quality care, and makes health insurance work against the sick.

More than that, however, this book is about how to fix those failed policies. Few voters or lawmakers have time to immerse themselves in a subject as complex as health policy. This book offers a quick guide to reforms that would make health care better, more affordable, and more secure—particularly for the most vulnerable patients.

You may enjoy reading it cover to cover. Or just select chapters. Chapters 2–4 introduce some of the successes and failures of the U.S. health care sector. Chapters 5–13 detail the reforms that state and federal officials must enact to make health care work for all patients. Chapter 14 hopes to motivate policymakers to enact these reforms.

2. WHAT THE U.S. HEALTH SECTOR DOES WELL

The U.S. health sector is exceptional—or maybe notorious—for the vast quantity of resources it consumes. U.S. residents spend more on health care than residents of any other nation.

- In 2021, health spending in the United States reached $12,318 per person. That's more than double Canada's figure ($5,905). It is 67 percent higher than second-place Germany ($7,383).[1]
- U.S. residents spent 18 percent of gross domestic product (GDP) on health in 2021. That's a larger share of the economy than any other nation. Germany was a distant second at 13 percent of GDP.[2]
- In 2021, the U.S. health sector consumed more resources ($4.3 trillion[3]) than the entire nation of France produced ($3.4 trillion[4]).
- Only five nations had total economic output that exceeded U.S. health spending: China ($24.3 trillion), India ($9.7 trillion), Japan ($5.4 trillion), Germany ($4.9 trillion), and Russia ($4.4 trillion).[5]

Those numbers are startling. But should they be? Is it really that bad to spend so much on health care? If each dollar of health spending were delivering greater benefits than it would elsewhere, U.S. residents might want to spend even *more* on health. The real issue is not how much U.S. residents spend on health care. The real issue is what they are getting in return.

On some margins, they get a lot in return. In corners of the U.S. health care sector where market forces have had room to breathe, innovations have made health care better, more affordable, and more secure, including for the most vulnerable patients. A few examples illustrate.

New Cures

The United States produces more valuable medical treatments and diagnostic tools than any other nation.[6] One of those innovations is the antiviral drug sofosbuvir.

Hepatitis C is a virus that damages the liver. It can result in liver failure, cirrhosis, cancer, and death. Researchers estimate that, worldwide, 58 million people have chronic hepatitis C infections and 290,000 people die from hepatitis C each year.[7] In the United States, there are approximately 2.5 million to 4.7 million people with chronic hepatitis C infections.[8]

Sofosbuvir, which goes by the brand name Sovaldi, is an "almost universal cure of chronic hepatitis C."[9] It has a cure rate between 84 percent to 96 percent.[10] One study found sofosbuvir reduced all-cause mortality among hepatitis C patients by more than 50 percent.[11]

New treatments like sofosbuvir make health care more universal. Prior to its development, there was no cure for hepatitis C. Around the world, hepatitis C patients were falling through this very large crack in their nations' supposedly universal health systems. Since sofosbuvir's introduction in 2014, this miracle cure has been saving lives not just in the United States, but in nations around the world. By developing sofosbuvir, the U.S. health sector made health care more universal everywhere—including in countries that supposedly already had universal health care.

Innovative Health Insurance Plans

Similarly, the U.S. health sector has developed innovative health care systems that solve what might otherwise be intractable problems. Integrated, prepaid group health plans like Kaiser Permanente are market innovations that date back as far as 150 years.[12] These systems excel on many dimensions of quality where the U.S. health sector is weak. Such systems

- offer conveniences like electronic communications, scheduling, and records, on which the rest of the U.S. health sector lags;
- coordinate the care each patient receives and offer a single point of payment and accountability;
- encourage higher-quality, lower-cost care, such as when Group Health Cooperative of Puget Sound improved the health of Type 2 diabetics, achieving "better glycemic control [with] average cost savings . . . of $685–$950 per patient per year";[13]
- encourage safer medicine by making health care providers bear the financial costs of medical errors.

Integrated, prepaid group plans can even perform functions that government has stripped from the private sector. After the U.S. Food and Drug Administration (FDA) approved the nonsteroidal anti-inflammatory (NSAID) drug rofecoxib (brand name: Vioxx) as safe, critics began to suspect the drug was nevertheless causing heart attacks. Kaiser Permanente was able to do what

Figure 2.1
Kaiser Permanente advertised its unique ability to identify unsafe drugs

Source: Kaiser Permanente Thrive, "Electronic Health Records Enabled Kaiser Permanente to Identify Vioxx Concerns," July 26, 2018, YouTube video.

neither the FDA nor the drug's manufacturer Merck could: provide data on outcomes for rofecoxib and other NSAIDs for 1.4 million adults—results that established rofecoxib does in fact increase the risk of serious coronary heart disease.[14] Kaiser boasted about its role in saving lives the same way other businesses boast about their quality advantages (see Figure 2.1).

Just like Kaiser Permanente determined the (un)safety of a drug that was already on the market, such systems are able to conduct forward-looking, randomized, controlled studies to determine (and put their seal of approval on) the safety and efficacy of new drugs. Unlike the FDA's approach to certifying drug safety and efficacy (see Chapter 7), integrated, prepaid plans can provide this service in a way that respects the right of patients to make their own health decisions.

More Affordable Medical Care

Entrepreneurs in the United States are constantly developing ways to make medical care more affordable by producing the same or greater output with fewer inputs. One way they do so is by using lower-cost mid-level clinicians—such as nurse practitioners and physician assistants—to perform tasks that traditionally only higher-cost physicians performed.

- Retail clinics, such as CVS's MinuteClinic, make greater use of nurse practitioners and other midlevel clinicians, which enables them to offer primary care for around 30 percent less than what physician offices charge.[15]
- In 2019, a suburban Chicago health system replaced 15 physicians with nurse practitioners. Administrators explained, "Patients have made it very clear that they want less costly care and convenient access for . . . sore throats, rashes, earaches[,] which are the vast majority of cases we treat" in many of that system's facilities. One of the physicians who lost their jobs admitted, "There definitely is a good share of lower-acuity things, which I think would be fine for a nurse practitioner to see."[16]
- From 2008 to 2016, the share of specialty practices that employ either nurse practitioners or physician assistants grew from 23 percent to 28 percent, while the share of primary care practices that do so increased from 28 percent to 35 percent.[17]
- With special training, midlevel clinicians can even reduce the cost of more complex services. The state of Oregon recently removed the legal barriers that had prevented competent nurse practitioners from performing vasectomies.[18]

Research indicates that when midlevel clinicians provide services within the scope of their training, they perform as well as physicians do on quality and beat physicians on cost.[19] In 2020, for example, researchers published a study of 800,000 patients who received plausibly random assignment to nurse practitioners or physicians. The study found that nurse practitioners delivered comparable outcomes to physicians.[20] Integrated, prepaid group health plans in particular make greater use of midlevel clinicians.

Innovators are also reducing costs by providing services in less-costly settings. Ambulatory surgical centers perform cataract surgeries for roughly $1,000, about half of the price in hospital outpatient departments.[21]

Monopoly-Busting Insurance Designs

Innovators have developed insurance features that reduce prices for cataract surgeries and other common procedures by thousands or even tens of thousands of dollars.[22]

Under one such innovation—a "reverse deductible"—patients can use any health care provider they wish and the insurer pays the same fixed amount per procedure, no matter which provider the patient chooses.[23] If the provider charges more than that fixed amount, the patient pays the balance.[24] Multiple experiments have found that when consumers face 100 percent of the marginal

Figure 2.2
Price-conscious patients lower prices: Average price reductions within two years of patients becoming price-conscious

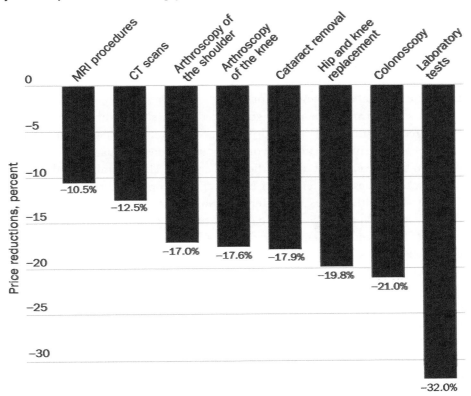

Source: James Robinson, Timothy Brown, and Christopher Whaley, "Reference Pricing Changes the 'Choice Architecture' of Health Care for Consumers," *Health Affairs* 36, no. 3 (March 2017): 524–30.

cost of the services they receive, they demand price transparency and change their behavior by switching to lower-cost providers.

What's more, price-conscious consumers changed *providers'* behavior by forcing them to reduce their prices. In just two years, reverse deductibles drove providers to reduce prices for colonoscopies by an average $360 (21 percent); for knee arthroscopy by more than $1,000 (18 percent); for cataract removal by $1,019 (45 percent); for shoulder arthroscopy by $1,336 (17 percent); and for hip and knee replacements by $9,000 (20 percent).[25] (See Figure 2.2.) Hospitals that had been charging the most for joint replacements cut their prices by an average $16,000, or 37 percent per procedure. Innovation allowed price-conscious patients to do what insurers could not do themselves: overcome the market power of monopolistic hospitals.

Secure Health Insurance

Innovators have even made health insurance more secure. They have developed innovative health insurance products such as "renewal guarantees" that allow patients with expensive conditions like diabetes, heart disease, or cancer to keep purchasing insurance at standard rates. "Before the passage of Medicare" in 1965, 72 insurance companies offered guaranteed-renewable health insurance and "many Americans over sixty-five were covered by health insurance policies that were guaranteed renewable for life."[26]

Even as government penalized guaranteed-renewable health insurance and subsidized substitutes for it, health insurance markets didn't stop innovating. In 2009, one private insurance company used renewal guarantees to fix a problem that government intervention had created. The federal tax code penalizes workers unless they enroll in employer-sponsored health insurance (see Chapter 10), which does not offer renewal guarantees. UnitedHealthcare received approval from 25 states to offered renewal guarantees as a standalone product for workers with employer-sponsored health insurance. Those products guaranteed that workers who lose their employer-sponsored coverage could enroll in a health insurance plan of their choice, at healthy-person rates, even if they had developed an expensive condition in the meantime. What we might call "preexisting conditions insurance" cost one-fifth the price of the underlying health insurance policy.[27] Economists theorize that innovators could make health insurance even more secure by offering total-satisfaction guarantees.[28]

These and other innovations should be spreading throughout the economy like wildfire—expanding access, making health care simpler for patients to understand, getting the right medicine to the right patient, reducing medical errors, reducing the burden of disease, and saving lives.

3. WHERE THE U.S. HEALTH SECTOR FAILS

Had government never stood in the way, by now nearly everyone would have electronic health records, utero-to-grave health insurance coverage, and countless other quality-improving and cost-reducing innovations. Unfortunately, government has put an end to those and other innovations. The result is that health care has become increasingly less affordable while patients suffer from an epidemic of low-quality medical care.

An Epidemic of Low-Quality Care

Many of the U.S. health sector's quality failings are obvious to patients. The sector lags behind other sectors in providing basic conveniences like electronic scheduling, records, and communications.

More frightening, and harder for patients to detect, is that the quality of medical care they receive is often so low as to be harmful to their health. Researchers estimate "perhaps well less than half" of all medical interventions that U.S. patients receive have reliable evidence demonstrating their effectiveness.[1] Studies find that health care providers persistently fail to recommend low-cost, highly effective treatments for numerous medical conditions.[2] Decades of research have found, "We may be wasting perhaps 30 percent of U.S. health care spending on medical care that does not appear to improve our health" and that patients who receive excessive, wasteful services receive lower-quality care and have "a higher risk of death over time."[3]

Low-quality care jeopardizes patients' health. Researchers at Johns Hopkins University estimate that *preventable* medical errors cause 251,000 deaths annually.[4] Others put the figure as high as 400,000 preventable deaths.[5] If accurate, these estimates indicate low-quality medical care is perhaps the third- or fourth-leading cause of death in the United States after heart disease, cancer, and COVID-19 (which caused 351,000 deaths in 2020).[6] If these estimates are remotely accurate, low-quality medical care causes far more deaths each year than firearms (40,000/year) or a lack of health insurance (45,000/year under the highest estimates).[7]

Excessive Prices Threaten Access

Even when innovators find ways to reduce health care *costs*, health care *prices* remain excessive. "Prices of labor and goods, including pharmaceuticals, and administrative costs appear[] to be the major drivers of the difference in overall cost between the United States and other high-income countries."[8]

Prices for colonoscopies, knee and shoulder arthroscopy, hip and knee replacements, lab tests, MRIs, CT scans, cataract removals, glycemic control, primary care, vasectomies, and countless other medical goods and services remain too high because government blocks the innovations that would reduce those prices and bring health care within reach of more patients.[9] Chronicling all the ways the health care and health insurance industries overcharge consumers and taxpayers would require a book far longer than this one.[10]

Excessive Health Insurance Increases Prices

Health insurance exists to protect consumers from health care prices they could not otherwise afford. But in the United States, government intervention simultaneously encourages excessive health insurance, which contributes to the problem of excessive health care prices, and makes health insurance less secure, which in turn exposes consumers to those excessive prices when they can least afford them.

Experiments with reverse deductibles (see Chapter 2) illustrate empirically what economists have argued for decades: health insurance increases health care prices, and excessive health insurance leads to excessive health care prices. Patients simply don't scrutinize prices when someone else is paying the way they do when they are picking up the tab themselves. When government encourages excessive coverage levels (see Chapter 10), that lack of scrutiny allows health care providers to charge excessive prices.

Insecure Health Insurance

As if that weren't bad enough, government intervention in health insurance markets routinely causes U.S. consumers to lose their coverage for no good reason, which then unnecessarily exposes consumers to those excessive prices. Secure health insurance would stay with the policyholder through all of life's changes. Yet government intervention causes U.S. patients to lose their coverage when

- they quit their jobs, lose their jobs, or just become too sick to work;
- their employer goes out of business, stops offering health benefits, switches health plans, or changes how much it pays for their benefits;

- they divorce or a spouse dies;
- they turn 19, or 26, or 65;
- the police arrest them (even if unlawfully);
- their income falls;
- their income rises; and/or
- their insurer makes the "mistake" of offering coverage that sick people want.

Without government intervention, some of those changes probably would cause some consumers to lose their coverage. Government intervention has guaranteed they will.

Even when government intervention hasn't (yet) thrown consumers out of their health insurance plans, it forces insurers to compete not to improve quality but to reduce the quality of coverage they provide to the sick. Government regulation literally penalizes insurers that offer quality health insurance to the sick, to the point that even "currently healthy consumers cannot be adequately insured."[11] Government intervention turns what otherwise would be adequate health insurance into junk plans.

4. EXTENSIVE GOVERNMENT CONTROL

According to some observers, in the United States, "health care is left mostly to the free market."[1] Some critics of the U.S. health sector allege that is the reason it so often fails patients. In health care, they argue, free markets inevitably produce excessive prices, insecure coverage, and low-quality care.

The idea that the U.S. health sector is a free market is absurd. The pathologies it exhibits occur not because markets are in charge but because government is. Consider the vast amount of control government wields over health spending in the United States.

Among advanced nations, the United States ranks near the top in terms of government control of health spending. The Organisation for Economic Co-operation and Development (OECD) collects data on 38 economically advanced nations.[2] The OECD reports that in the average member country, 76 percent of health spending is compulsory. That is, rather than allow consumer preferences to allocate those funds, government requires residents to allocate those funds according to the government's preferences or face penalties. In the United States, government controls a significantly *larger* share of health spending than the OECD average: 85 percent of U.S. health spending is compulsory. That's just 3 percentage points shy of the highest-ranking Czech Republic (88 percent). Government controls a larger share of health spending in the United States than in 30 other advanced nations, including Canada (75 percent) and the United Kingdom (83 percent), which have explicitly socialized health systems (see Figure 4.1).

Another indicator of how the U.S. health sector diverges from a free market is that government compels U.S. residents to devote a larger share of the economy to health spending than other nations' governments do. As a share of GDP, compulsory health spending in the United States exceeds *total* health spending in every other OECD nation (see Figure 4.2).[3]

Another way the U.S. health sector departs from a free market is that the federal government requires patients to obtain permission from government-appointed gatekeepers before purchasing certain medications. A 2009 study of government-imposed prescription requirements found the United States is even less of a free market in this regard than some other advanced nations.

Figure 4.1

Compulsory spending comprises a larger share of health spending in the United States than in most OECD nations, 2020

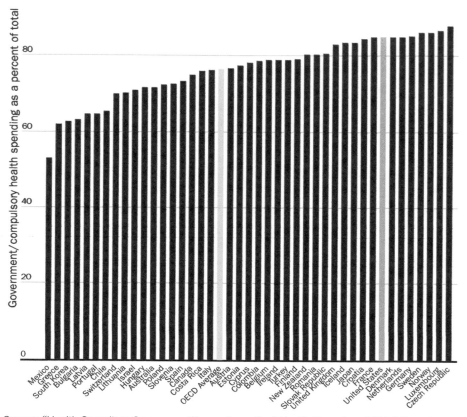

Source: "Health Spending: Government/Compulsory, % of Health Spending, 2020," Organisation for Economic Co-operation and Development.
Note: OECD = Organisation for Economic Co-operation and Development.

The U.S. government required a physician's permission to purchase nearly twice as many of 86 select pharmaceutical products as Australia's government did: 42 versus 23.[4] (See Figure 4.3.)

Control over health spending and government-imposed barriers to accessing medication are just two ways government blocks the market forces of individual choice, innovation, and competition that would otherwise make health care better, more affordable, and more secure. This book examines only the most harmful of those measures. To chronicle all of them would require several books.

Figure 4.2
Government compels U.S. residents to spend a larger share of GDP on health care than residents of other OECD nations, 2020

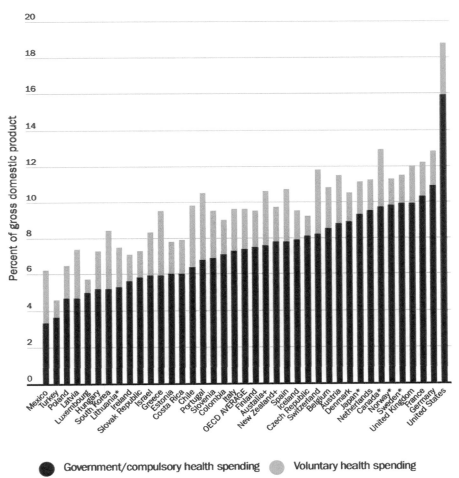

● Government/compulsory health spending ● Voluntary health spending

Source: "Health Spending: Total/Government/Compulsory, % of GDP, 2020" Organisation for Economic Co-operation and Development, https://data.oecd.org/chart/6Lr9.
Notes: GDP = gross domestic product; OECD = Organisation for Economic Co-operation and Development; * = provisional data; + = estimated data.

A Ray of Hope

The good news is that, in corners of the U.S. health sector where market forces have had room to breathe, they have developed the above innovations and more—often despite government policies that inhibit them or that exist

Figure 4.3
Government-imposed barriers to access for 86 pharmaceuticals across 5 countries, grouped by type of permission required, 2009

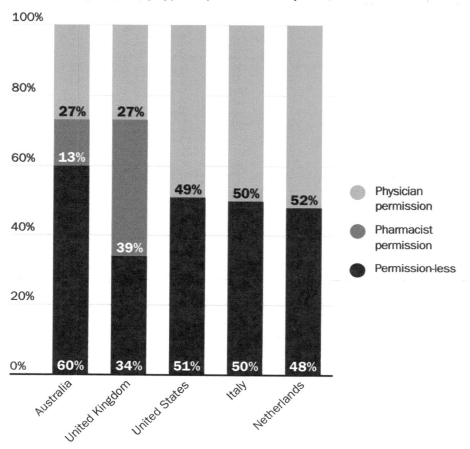

Source: U.S. Government Accountability Office and author's categories.

explicitly to block them. Those successes provide evidence that free markets can deliver better, more affordable, and more secure health care than any alternative system.

These innovations should be exploding across the country and the world, making medical care more affordable for low-income patients and driving high-cost/low-quality providers and insurers out of business. But they aren't.

Markets developed integrated, prepaid group plans more than a century ago. Yet government has been blocking such plans, and the cost and quality improvements they offer, for just as long. Many state legislatures enacted laws explicitly prohibiting these plans. Government licensing of clinicians and insurers inhibits their creation and growth. Even where integrated, prepaid systems have broken through those barriers, consumers are still not free to choose them because government penalizes workers who choose health plans other than what their employer offers. Congress denies prepaid group plans a competitive advantage they would otherwise enjoy by granting the FDA a monopoly over safety and efficacy certification for new drugs and medical devices. The list goes on. Had government never stood in the way of integrated, prepaid group plans, we would all have electronic medical records and countless other innovations by now—even if we enrolled in different types of plans.

The net effect of all the ways government blocks consumer-friendly innovations is that U.S. consumers are suffering under a ridiculously cruel system of high and opaque prices, low-quality and inconvenient care, and shaky health insurance. This system persists *solely* because government is actively protecting from competition countless high-cost, low-quality providers and insurers who would never survive in a market system.

Bringing quality medical care to patients who need it requires breaking down the barriers government puts in the way of better, more affordable care. The following chapters explain how to make that a reality.

5. CLINICIANS

States should

- eliminate government licensing of medical professionals;
- or, as preliminary steps, recognize licenses from other states and third-party credentialing organizations; and
- eliminate price controls, including "parity" laws for telehealth and other services.

Congress should

- eliminate states' ability to use licensing laws as a barrier to entry by medical professionals who hold licenses from other states.

The most important health care right is the right to make one's own health decisions. When government regulations deny consumers their choice of providers and treatments, or when government refuses to enforce certain contracts, it violates patients' rights to make their own health decisions and reduces access to care.

Making health care better, more affordable, and more secure, particularly for the most vulnerable, requires restoring and protecting those rights. Policymakers must eliminate regulations that deny consumers the right to make their own health decisions and must honor contracts between competent patients and providers.

End Government Licensing of Medical Professionals

Government licensing of clinicians violates the right of patients to choose their providers, makes health care less accessible by increasing prices, and reduces the quality of medical care.

Markets make medical care more affordable in part by allowing competent clinicians with less training than physicians, such as nurse practitioners and physician assistants, to perform progressively more tasks.[1] Markets improve quality in part by allowing clinicians to combine their skills in various ways. Among the quality-improving innovations that markets have produced are integrated group health plans that coordinate care and offer other efficiencies. Patients have a right to choose to receive medical care from independent nurse practitioners, integrated group plans, or any other arrangement entrepreneurs offer.

Clinician licensing blocks entry by these and other providers. It therefore blocks the market processes that make health care better, more affordable, and more secure.

To practice medicine in a state, clinicians—physicians, nurse practitioners, physician assistants, dentists, dental hygienists, and others—must obtain a license from that state. Each state defines which clinician categories may exist. The states mandate minimum educational requirements for each profession. They define the list of tasks, or "scope of practice," that each license allows members of that profession to perform. States delegate these highly technical decisions to members of the health professions—typically physicians or dentists, who have the greatest understanding of the science of medicine and dentistry.

These are not scientific decisions. If they were, all states would have identical rules. Instead, state licensing laws vary dramatically on whether they allow nurse practitioners to prescribe medication (see Figure 5.1) or practice independently (see Figure 5.2), whether they allow dental therapists to practice at all (see Figure 5.3), and other dimensions of medical and dental practice.

Licensing gives self-interested incumbents—typically, physicians and dentists—the power to set rules for new entrants into their own profession and other health professions. In other words, it empowers incumbent clinicians to create barriers to entry for their competitors.

It should come as no surprise, therefore, that licensing typically leads to "steadily rising requirements" for entry into the health professions and that incumbents use licensing laws to block their competitors from providing particular services.[2] The American Medical Association, which lobbies on behalf of physicians, boasts that it has blocked more than 100 attempts to expand midlevel clinicians' scopes of practice since 2019.[3]

Those barriers may prevent some incompetent clinicians from entering the market and thereby protect some patients from low-quality care. That is the ostensible purpose of such laws.

Yet clinician licensing also reduces access to quality care in several ways. First, it increases prices. Licensing increases prices within each profession by increasing the cost of entering that profession. "As you increase the cost of the license to practice medicine you increase the price at which medical service must be sold and you correspondingly decrease the number of people who can afford to buy this medical service."[4]

Figure 5.1
Prescriptive authority of nurse practitioners by state

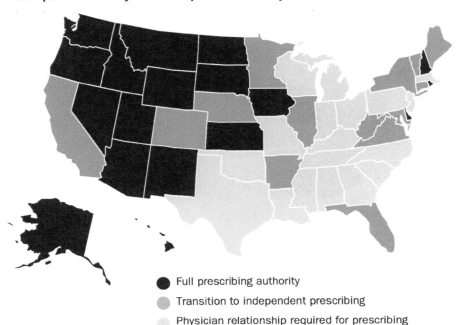

● Full prescribing authority
◔ Transition to independent prescribing
○ Physician relationship required for prescribing

Source: "Advanced Practice Registered Nurses: Nurse Practitioner Practice Authority," Scope of Practice Policy, National Conference of State Legislatures.

Licensing also increases prices by requiring patients to obtain services from more-expensive clinicians. Basic primary care generally costs 30 percent less in nurse practitioner–staffed retail clinics than in physicians' offices.[5] States that prohibit nurse practitioners from practicing independently (see Figure 5.2) require them to pay up to $15,000 annually to collaborate with a physician, which increases prices for those services.[6] The American Medical Association advocates such restrictions even as it grudgingly admits that midlevel clinicians can provide services within their training at a level of quality comparable to when physicians provide the same services.[7]

Finally, licensing increases prices by prohibiting many health professions outright. Only 14 states allow dental therapists to practice at all (see Figure 5.3). Patients in the remaining states must see higher-cost dentists for the same services.

Second, licensing blocks access to quality care by reducing the supply of high-quality providers as well as low-quality providers. Licensing may actually reduce the average quality of medical care by inhibiting higher-quality forms of health care delivery.

Figure 5.2
Independent-practice restrictions on nurse practitioners by state

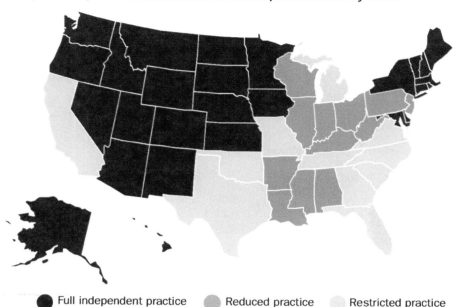

● Full independent practice   ● Reduced practice   ● Restricted practice

Source: "State Practice Environment," American Association of Nurse Practitioners, last updated October 2022.

Licensing blocks free medical care for the poor. The charitable organization Remote Area Medical (RAM) has turned away thousands of patients in need because licensing laws blocked highly qualified volunteer clinicians from around the country from practicing in states where RAM held clinics.[8] "RAM treated 7,000 patients in one week in Los Angeles, but turned away thousands more due to a shortage of California-licensed volunteers."[9] After a tornado struck Missouri in 2011, RAM "went to Joplin, Mo., with a mobile eyeglass lab. But they were not allowed to make free glasses because their volunteer optometrists and opticians were not licensed in the state."[10] Licensing often prevents such organizations from even holding clinics at all. RAM's late founder Stan Brock explained: "We've certainly talked to the New York authorities about holding one . . . in the Bronx. . . . But again the permission was denied on the licensing issue."[11] There is no quality-based argument for blocking clinicians with licenses from other states from providing free medical care to the poor.

Licensing blocks access to quality care by reducing the overall supply of clinicians, leaving many patients without access to care at all. Between 1900 and 1930, shortly after states began controlling entry into the medical profession,

Figure 5.3
Status of dental therapists by state

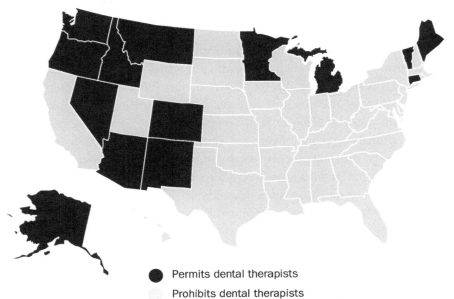

● Permits dental therapists
○ Prohibits dental therapists

Source: "Oral Health Providers: Dental Therapists," Scope of Practice Policy, National Conference of State Legislatures.

the number of physicians per capita fell by 28 percent.[12] One analysis found that "more than a third of 910 small towns that had physicians in 1914 had been abandoned by doctors by 1925." It was not just low-quality doctors that licensing blocked from the profession. As licensing laws took effect over this period, "the high costs of medical education and more stringent requirements limited the entry of students from the lower and working classes." Licensing boards closed many medical schools, including five of only seven historically black medical schools. The artificial shortage of medical school slots facilitated discrimination against immigrants, African Americans, women, and Jews in admissions.[13] It should go without saying that preventing these groups from entering the profession has nothing to do with improving quality and instead reduced quality.[14] The legacy of such quality-reducing discrimination persists to this day.

Licensing blocks access to the highest-quality providers in the country, forcing patients to settle for whatever clinicians happen to hold a license in their state. Patients have a right to travel to receive treatment from top specialists at the Cleveland Clinic, Memorial Sloan Kettering Cancer Center, the Mayo

Clinic, or other leading medical centers across the country. Licensing denies patients their right to consult those same clinicians via telehealth without leaving home.

Licensing reduces access to high-quality care by blocking entry from integrated, prepaid group plans like Kaiser Permanente. Such systems are strong on dimensions of quality such as coordinating care, conducting comparative-effectiveness research, and offering conveniences like electronic communications, scheduling, and medical records.[15] Many consumers appreciate and embrace this model.[16] Such systems compete on price by making fuller use of midlevel clinicians. Scope-of-practice restrictions disproportionately hinder such systems by depriving them of a key competitive advantage and by requiring them to develop new workflows to conform to each state's different and ever-changing scope-of-practice rules. Incumbent physicians have even stripped licenses from the physician who founded Kaiser Permanente and others whose only crime was to found or participate in similar plans across the country. The legacy of such discrimination also persists.[17]

States use licensing laws to restrict access to care for reasons that have nothing to do with quality.[18] Some 15 states reduce the supply of clinicians by revoking the licenses of clinicians who default on student loans.[19]

Finally, licensing does little to discipline clinicians who actually harm patients. A study by the consumer watchdog Public Citizen found that between 1990 and 2005, "only 33.26 percent of doctors who made 10 or more malpractice payments were disciplined by their state board—meaning two-thirds of doctors in this group of egregious repeat offenders were not disciplined at all."[20]

Licensing does more to protect the incomes of incumbent clinicians than to protect patients from low-quality care. It adds little if anything to the protections that the medical malpractice liability system and market forces provide. In the absence of clinician licensing, courts would continue to hold individual clinicians and health care organizations accountable for the harm they cause. Hospitals, health plans, and other organizations would continue to evaluate the competence of clinicians via board certification, private credentialing organizations, and their own internal processes.

In the absence of clinician licensing, market forces could provide even greater quality protections. Eliminating licensing would allow greater innovation and competition in health care delivery. Integrated, prepaid group plans could improve quality directly through greater care coordination and health services research. Greater demand for private credentialing and the desire to protect brand names and reputations together would do more than licensing does to safeguard patients from incompetent providers.

Repeal Medical Licensing

Clinician-licensing laws are a mistake that has done enormous harm to patients. Mere tinkering cannot fix them. Government cannot insulate such laws from the influence of incumbent clinicians. Even if it could, government would remain incapable of striking a proper balance between access and safety for millions of patients across billions of medical encounters.

State governments should repeal clinician-licensing laws. At a minimum, states should recognize clinician licenses from other states and other third-party credentialing organizations.

Repealing clinician licensing would reduce the cost of medical care while improving quality. In the absence of licensing, innovators would develop new ways to use midlevel clinicians. Consumers would benefit from greater choice and competition among different delivery and payment systems. Prices would fall for everything from medical education, primary, specialty, and hospital care to health insurance. Repealing licensing would bring health insurance and medical care within reach of many more low-income Americans. It would reduce the number of patients who cannot afford the care they need and reduce the cost of subsidizing those who remain.

Entry by new, higher-quality delivery systems, along with the health services research and competition they would generate, would improve quality. Such competition would add to the quality assurance mechanisms that would continue to operate in the absence of licensing, including the medical malpractice liability system, board certification, and private credentialing organizations. If repealing clinician licensing is politically infeasible, policymakers must stop licensing laws from acting as a barrier to entry for clinicians licensed by other states.

States must stop licensing from blocking free charitable care for the poor. RAM founder Brock wrote, "In the United States . . . for some extraordinary reason, practitioners educated and licensed in one state are not allowed to cross state lines to provide free care for needy Americans."[21] States should enact Good Samaritan laws like those that Connecticut, Illinois, Missouri, and Tennessee pioneered to allow clinicians from other states to give away free medical care to the poor. As Brock once testified: "One of the saddest parts of trying to help these people is on the last day of a free RAM event we always have to tell some of them we are sorry, but we cannot see any more patients. . . . If the government would allow willing volunteer practitioners to cross state lines, fewer people will be turned away."[22] Volunteer clinicians would still be liable for malpractice under the laws of the patient's state or the contractual liability rules the patient and clinicians agree to honor.

States must give rural and other patients access to top specialists by recognizing the licenses of telehealth providers in other states. One way to do so is to redefine the location of care from that of the patient to that of the provider—that is, the state where the provider already holds a license.

States can accomplish both of those reforms at once by recognizing clinician licenses from all other states. Arizona has enacted a law that greatly reduces the barriers to out-of-state clinicians practicing in the state.

Congress can use its power under the Commerce Clause to promote telehealth by redefining the location of the practice of medicine to be that of the clinician.

6. MEDICAL FACILITIES

States should

• eliminate "certificate of need" laws.

Markets also make medical care better, cheaper, and safer through competition between medical facilities—between retail clinics and physician offices; between urgent care clinics and hospital emergency departments; between standalone imaging centers, radiology practices, and hospital imaging facilities; and between ambulatory surgical centers, specialty hospitals, and general hospitals.

Many states impose laws requiring hospitals, nursing homes, and even physician offices to obtain a "certificate of need" (CON) from a state planning agency before opening or expanding a medical facility or investing in new equipment. CON laws violate the right of patients to choose which medical facilities they patronize. They are a leading barrier to the sort of competition that reduces prices and improves quality.

The rationale for CON laws is that by restraining the supply of hospital beds, the government could restrain medical spending. In 1974, the federal government encouraged states to adopt CON planning.

CON laws failed to slow the growth of medical spending. In a survey of the empirical literature on CON laws, health economist Michael Morrisey writes that those studies "find virtually no cost-containment effects. . . . If anything, CON programs tended to increase costs."[1] The failure of CON laws to achieve their stated aims led the federal government to lift its CON-planning requirement in 1987 and also led many states to eliminate their laws. Yet many states have maintained and even expanded their CON requirements.

Nor do CON laws appear to have increased the quality of care. Examining cost and outcomes data for coronary artery bypass grafts, economists Vivian Ho and Meei-Hsiang Ku-Goto found, "CON regulations . . . may not be justified in terms of either improving quality or controlling cost growth."[2]

Physician-economist Daniel Polsky and colleagues found that laws imposing CON on home-health agencies have "negligible" effects on quality or costs.[3]

Repeal Incumbent-Veto Laws

Perhaps because CON laws have done nothing to contain spending, they have been a boon for incumbent health care providers. Like clinician-licensing laws, CON laws empower incumbents to block new entrants and thereby protect themselves from competition. Morrisey explains:

> A reasonably large body of evidence suggests that CON has been used to the benefit of existing hospitals. Prices and costs were higher in the presence of CON, investor-owned hospitals were less likely to enter the market, multi-hospital systems were less likely to be formed, and hospitals were less likely to be managed under for-profit contract. . . . The continued existence of CON and, indeed, its reintroduction and expansion despite overwhelming evidence of its ineffectiveness as a cost-control device suggest that something other than the public interest is being sought. The provider self-interest view is worthy of examination.[4]

Indeed, when new entrants apply for certificates of need, incumbent hospitals and other providers object the loudest. Law professor Sallyanne Payton and physician Rhoda M. Powsner explain that although the stated rationale of CON laws is to reduce health care spending, this claim "has diverted attention from the actual economic and political imperatives that led to and presently sustain certificate-of-need regulation. To attribute CON legislation to [cost reduction] is to mistake a convenient theoretical justification for an actual motivation."[5]

States should eliminate CON laws immediately without any concessions to the inefficient incumbent providers they protect from competition. CON laws harm consumers and taxpayers by increasing health care prices without improving quality. They deny patients their right to choose their medical facilities and the benefits of new forms of health care delivery. There is no justification for them and no place in a market economy for such top-down economic planning.

State officials concerned about runaway health expenditures should reduce or eliminate the government subsidies that fuel such spending (see Chapters 10, 11, and 12).

7. DRUGS AND MEDICAL DEVICES

Congress should

- eliminate the U.S. Food and Drug Administration (FDA);
- or, as preliminary steps, eliminate premarket-approval requirements for drugs and medical devices;
- eliminate government-imposed prescription requirements for drugs and medical devices;
- eliminate the FDA's power to limit truthful speech; and
- recognize drug and device approvals by other third-party organizations, including foreign governments.

To market a drug or medical device in the United States, manufacturers must first prove to the satisfaction of the FDA that the product is safe and effective for the indication that will go on the product's label.

The FDA helps patients when it approves beneficial drugs and blocks harmful drugs. Yet the agency can also harm patients, by either approving harmful drugs (a "Type I error") or denying approval to beneficial drugs (a "Type II error"). Both Type I and Type II errors can cause suffering and death. Economist Ernst Berndt writes, "A central tradeoff facing the FDA involves balancing its two goals—protecting public health by assuring the safety and efficacy of drugs, and advancing the public health by helping to secure and speed access to new innovations."[1]

The tradeoff between the number of harmful drugs the FDA approves and the number of beneficial drugs it delays or rejects—that is, between Type I and Type II errors—is unavoidable. Reducing the number of harmful drugs (Type I errors) requires higher standards of evidence, more testing, more time, and more expense. Those measures necessarily increase the number of beneficial drugs the FDA delays or rejects, and they reduce the number of beneficial drugs that manufacturers develop (Type II errors). Conversely, reducing the number of beneficial drugs the FDA delays or rejects (Type II errors) requires

Table 7.1
The Food and Drug Administration's asymmetric information problem

FDA decision	Helpful drug	Harmful drug
Approve	Patients benefit.	Patients suffer. Victims/others *can* trace injury to FDA officials.
Delay/reject	Patients suffer. Victims/others *cannot* trace injury to FDA officials.	Patients benefit.

Note: FDA = Food and Drug Administration.

easing those barriers to market entry, which inevitably leads to the approval of a greater number of harmful drugs (Type I errors).

As an agency that responds to Congress rather than to patients, the FDA faces an inherent information problem that inevitably leads to unnecessary suffering and death. Though Type I and Type II errors can be equally dangerous, Table 7.1 illustrates a very important difference from the FDA's perspective. The political system penalizes FDA officials when a patient dies from a harmful drug the officials approved (Type I error). It penalizes agency officials far less often when a patient dies because they blocked or discouraged the development of a beneficial drug (Type II error).

- **Type I errors** bring swift and certain retribution down on agency officials. The victims are easily identifiable. Patients and the public can easily trace the victims' injuries to the FDA's decision. The victims, their loved ones, the media, and Congress can hold FDA officials to account for approving a harmful product. Importantly, FDA officials *know* Type I errors lead to congressional hearings, public disgrace, and possibly the end of their careers.
- **Type II errors** bring almost no consequences for FDA officials. Even though delaying or blocking beneficial drugs can harm patients as much as approving unsafe drugs can, it is typically impossible to hold FDA officials to account for Type II errors. Victims of Type II errors are much harder to identify. It appears the disease, not the FDA, killed them. Typically, neither the victims, nor their loved ones, nor FDA officials can identify which patients an unapproved but beneficial drug might have helped. Victims and their families may never have heard of the drug, perhaps because the high cost of FDA approval deterred companies from ever developing it.

Due to this fundamental information asymmetry, the political system can discipline FDA officials only when their decisions cause patients to suffer or die from Type I errors. It effectively cannot discipline FDA officials when their decisions cause patients to suffer and die from Type II errors. Dr. Henry Miller, a former FDA official, describes how this information asymmetry affects the decisions of FDA officials:

> In the early 1980s, when I headed the team at the FDA that was reviewing the [new drug application] for recombinant human insulin, the first drug made with gene-splicing techniques, we were ready to recommend approval a mere four months after the application was submitted (at a time when the average time for [new drug application] review was more than two and a half years). . . . My supervisor refused to sign off on the approval—even though he agreed that the data provided compelling evidence of the drug's safety and effectiveness. "If anything goes wrong," he argued, "think how bad it will look that we approved the drug so quickly.". . . The supervisor was more concerned with not looking bad in case of an unforeseen mishap than with getting an important new product to patients who needed it.[2]

As a result of this information problem and the perverse incentives it creates, the FDA typically tolerates only a 2.5 percent chance of Type I error when determining whether to approve new drugs. Biostatistician Leah Isakov and colleagues estimate that if the agency's goal is to save lives, it should be much more tolerant of Type I errors. They estimate that for hypertensive disease, the agency should tolerate a 7.6–9.4 percent chance of Type I errors. For cirrhosis of the liver, it should tolerate a 15.3–17.7 percent chance. For pancreatic cancer, it should tolerate as much as a 27.8 percent chance.[3]

Indeed, cost–benefit analyses consistently find that, at the margin, FDA regulation on balance *harms* patients' health.

- Economist Mary K. Olson estimates that when additional revenue from user fees enabled the FDA to review drugs more quickly, the health benefits of quicker access to new drugs were roughly 12 times greater than the costs from additional adverse drug reactions.[4] In other words, the FDA was inflicting 12 times as much harm on patients through Type II errors as it was sparing patients by avoiding Type I errors.
- Economist Tomas Philipson and colleagues found that quicker reviews "saved the equivalent of [up to] 310,000 life years" while drugs "subsequently withdrawn for safety reasons" during this period were responsible for at most 56,000 life years lost. This study suggests the FDA was inflicting 5.5 times as much harm on patients through Type II errors as it was preventing by avoiding Type I errors.[5]

Market-based safety and efficacy certification would save more lives by striking a better balance between Type I and Type II errors. No one would have the power to force patients to suffer Type II errors. Market-based certification respects the freedom of doctors and patients to make treatment decisions according to individual circumstances.

If FDA officials want to promote health, they should regulate less. They should approve new drugs faster and with less evidence of safety and effectiveness. Unfortunately, this information asymmetry affects more than just the FDA. Despite such research, many in Congress have sought to give the FDA additional powers to reduce Type I errors.

Government-Imposed Prescription Requirements

Congress also empowers the FDA to determine whether consumers must obtain a prescription before accessing certain drugs. Government-imposed prescription requirements violate the rights of individuals to make their own health decisions. Here again, the agency's incentives routinely lead it to impose rules that on balance harm rather than protect patients.

The FDA has used its power to impose prescription requirements to steer consumers toward *more* dangerous drugs. For years, the agency required prescriptions for nonsedating antihistamines while allowing over-the-counter access to sedating antihistamines, a policy that likely caused air- and auto-travel crashes and fatalities. The FDA blocked access to "Plan B" emergency contraception for more than 12 years. FDA-imposed prescription requirements continue to block access to routine-use oral contraceptives—which are available without prescription in more than 100 countries—and to life-saving drugs such as naloxone.

Government-imposed prescription requirements make patients less safe, not more safe. Economist Sam Peltzman found:

- "Enforcement of prescription regulation *increases* poisoning mortality by 50 to 100 percent";[6]
- "No . . . statistically significant difference in infectious disease mortality between countries that enforce prescription requirements for antibiotics and those that do not";[7] and
- "[Prescription] regulation did not reduce—indeed, may have increased—poisoning mortality from drug consumption . . . poisoning mortality is higher, all else remaining the same, in countries that enforce prescription regulation."[8]

Medical historian Harry Marks noted, "the FDA would instruct firms to remove from their labels any remaining information that might guide lay users of prescription drugs."[9] Economist Peter Temin therefore argues that "some part of the gap between the drug knowledge of the average doctor and the average consumer is the product of regulation."[10] Public health professor Julie Donohue notes giving the FDA this power created "a paradoxical situation . . . in which potentially dangerous prescription drugs were dispensed to consumers with less accompanying information than [over-the-counter] drugs carried."[11]

A Better Way to Certify and Monitor Drugs and Medical Devices

The FDA's asymmetric information problem will always lead the agency to value some lives more than others and tolerate unnecessary suffering and death. Fortunately, there is a voluntary, market-based alternative that does not suffer from that information problem and that respects the right of patients to make their own medical decisions.

Nobel Prize–winning economist Gary Becker advocated eliminating the FDA's efficacy standard and returning the agency to the *status quo ante* 1962, when the FDA only had the power to block drugs it believed to be unsafe. Peltzman argues that even the safety requirement delivers more harm than benefit. Another Nobel Prize–winning economist, Milton Friedman, proposed eliminating the FDA entirely. As long as a government agency exists whose purpose is to protect patients from harmful drugs, it will always focus disproportionately on Type I errors at the expense of overall patient health. Congress should eliminate any role for the federal government in certifying the safety and efficacy of drugs or in determining which drugs consumers should need prescriptions to purchase.

Eliminating the FDA would increase patient demand for private certification of safety and efficacy, which currently exists but only informally. The threat of liability for harmful products would create powerful incentives for pharmaceutical manufacturers to conduct appropriate testing and seek private certification.

Integrated, prepaid group plans like Kaiser Permanente are uniquely capable of performing safety and efficacy certification. When the FDA wanted to determine whether the pain reliever Vioxx—which it had approved—was causing heart attacks, the agency could not conduct that research itself. It turned to Kaiser Permanente of Northern and Southern California. With liberalization of clinician-licensing laws and reforms that allow consumers to control their health spending (see Chapters 10 and 11), additional integrated, prepaid plans could enter the market and offer competing safety and efficacy certifications. Different plans would cater to different risk preferences by applying different approval requirements. Each plan's reputation for quality—and ability to attract enrollees—would depend on the perceived value of its seal of approval. Patients within or outside such plans would rely on whichever plan's seal of approval fit their own risk preferences. Unlike the FDA, prepaid group plans could consider cost-effectiveness as a criterion for approval. Unlike the FDA, they could closely monitor drug safety and efficacy after approval and could more quickly detect adverse drug reactions.

An important step toward reforming the regulation of drugs and medical devices therefore is to eliminate the barriers that Congress and state legislatures have erected to integrated, prepaid group plans (see Chapters 5, 6, 9, 10, and 11).

Concurrently, Congress could allow alternative ways of certifying the safety and efficacy of medical products by granting marketing approval to products that other countries' regulatory bodies approve.

The next step would be to eliminate either the efficacy standard or the FDA entirely. Either would save lives, on balance, because patients would get quicker access to more beneficial new drugs. While patients would also have quicker access to harmful drugs, at least three factors make that unfortunate effect tolerable. First, more patients would live and thrive thanks to greater innovation and quicker access to helpful drugs than would suffer as a result of harmful drugs. Second, eliminating either the efficacy standard or the FDA itself would lead to greater skepticism of new drugs by doctors and patients. Third, innovations by prepaid group plans and others would more quickly detect and stop adverse drug reactions.

8. MEDICAL MALPRACTICE LIABILITY

States should

- eliminate statutory caps on damages in medical malpractice cases; and
- direct courts to enforce private contracts in which patients and providers agree on alternative medical malpractice liability rules.

Congress should

- reject federal medical malpractice reforms.

The right to sue health care providers for medical malpractice is a crucial civil right. Individuals are not free to make their own health decisions if health care providers can impose costs on patients without their consent.

The right to sue for medical malpractice is also an important tool for protecting patients from injury due to negligent care. Patients typically have little information about the quality of care they receive. To the extent that the medical malpractice "system" imposes the costs of negligent care on providers, it encourages providers to take steps to improve quality.

Nevertheless, many people in the United States complain—with some justification—that this system performs poorly. "The medical malpractice system is slow, expensive . . . stressful to both sides, contentious, prone to error in both directions (i.e., payment for weak claims and nonpayment for strong claims), and perceived by everyone involved as inhumane."[1] According to one estimate, "it costs $1.33 in overhead to deliver $1 to negligently injured plaintiffs."[2] Even so, research suggests the system does not do enough to discourage negligent care. Physicians and other providers—who see often-dramatic increases in malpractice insurance premiums—have intermittently declared this system to be in crisis for more than 30 years.

Scholars have proposed various reforms. California and Texas have limited the amount patients can recover for noneconomic damages to $250,000 per injury.[3] Other proposals include

- legislative limits on contingency fees for plaintiffs' attorneys;
- "no-fault" compensation systems for medical injuries, such as the limited programs in Florida and Virginia;
- alternative forms of dispute resolution, such as arbitration and special medical courts;
- the English rule of costs ("loser pays"); and
- reform of the collateral source rule.

Each of these reforms would leave some patients better off—typically by reducing prices for medical care—at the cost of leaving other patients worse off. "Loser pays" reforms often reallocate the costs of frivolous lawsuits to the party who is in the wrong. However, that rule deters less affluent patients from seeking legal redress for legitimate grievances. Limits on contingency fees could expand access to medical care by reducing prices, but at the cost of denying compensation to injured patients whose cases those caps make it uprofitable for plaintiffs' attorneys to pursue. Perhaps most important, any reduction in provider liability potentially jeopardizes patient safety by reducing the incentives for providers to avoid negligent care.

In particular, caps on damages could expand access to health care by reducing payouts and liability insurance premiums, but at the cost of leaving some injured patients with uncompensated losses. Damage caps in California and Texas force patients to bear the cost of any noneconomic losses they suffer in excess of $250,000.[4]

Moreover, damage caps do not appear to solve the system's problems or even deliver on the promises of supporters (disproportionately, physicians) that caps will increase physician supply or reduce health care spending. A series of empirical studies by law professor Bernard Black and colleagues on Texas's damage caps concluded:

> Texas's damage cap dramatically reduced the number of medical malpractice cases and total payouts to plaintiffs, with an especially strong effect on elderly plaintiffs. But Texas's tort reform package had no discernible, favorable impact on broader measures of health system performance. Health care spending growth did not slow, and physician supply did not increase. . . . While reform strongly benefited providers, the evidence that it had significant benefits for the broader health care system is simply not there.[5]

Like clinician-licensing regulation, physician groups' proposals regarding medical malpractice liability benefit physicians at the expense of patients.

Many Republicans want Congress to enact nationwide limits on malpractice liability. The U.S. Constitution does not authorize Congress to impose substantive rules of tort law on the states. While the federal government may enact technical procedural changes to tort law, state legislatures are the proper venue for correcting excesses in their civil justice systems. The fact that medical professionals can avoid states with inhospitable civil justice systems gives them significant leverage when advocating state-level medical liability reforms and gives states incentives to enact such reforms. Indeed, many states have.

Though state action is preferable to federal action, state-imposed medical malpractice reforms share two flaws with federal reform. First, imposing on all patients and providers any single set of limits on the right to sue for medical malpractice will help some patients but hurt others. Second, while patients should be free to avoid harmful rules, making any single set of rules mandatory and codifying them in statute makes removing harmful rules extremely difficult.

A more patient-friendly and choice-enhancing approach would allow patients and providers to adopt their own medical malpractice reforms via legally enforceable contracts. For cases of ordinary negligence, patients could choose the level of protection they desire, rather than have government impose on them a uniform level of protection (and the accompanying price tag). Providers could offer discounts to patients who agree to limits on compensation in the event of an injury. Patients who don't agree could pay the higher, nondiscounted price or seek a better deal from another provider. This freedom to contract would thus make medical care more affordable to many low-income patients.

Insurance companies could facilitate such contracts on behalf of their enrollees. Those companies would have strong incentives to ensure that such contracts provide adequate protection; otherwise, the insurers could face higher claims from injured patients who could not collect the full extent of their damages.

Regular tort rules would continue to apply in cases where patients and providers could not or did not contract around them in advance, where patients were subject to duress, or where providers were guilty of intentional wrongdoing or reckless behavior.

Freedom of contract would also enhance quality competition. Providers who invest in processes that avoid patient injuries could offer equivalent or more expansive malpractice protections than their competitors at a lower price. Low-quality providers would not be able to do so, and would therefore face strong financial incentives to improve quality.

Such contracts are not possible today because courts have invalidated them as "contracts of adhesion" or "against public policy." The courts' refusal to honor those contracts restricts the freedom of adults to make mutually beneficial exchanges that hurt no one else. It also increases the price of providing medical care to the poor, which has undoubtedly reduced their access to care.

To remedy this undue and costly restriction on patient freedom, courts should abandon their current policy and enforce contractual limitations on the right to sue for medical malpractice. If courts refuse, state legislatures should require them to do so. Nobel Prize–winning economist Richard Thaler and law professor Cass Sunstein write:

> In our view, state lawmakers should think seriously about increasing freedom of contract in the domain of medical malpractice, if only to see whether such experiments would reduce the cost of health care without decreasing its quality. Increasing contractual freedom won't solve the health care crisis. But it might well help—and in this domain every little bit of help counts.[6]

The medical malpractice system does a poor job of providing relief to injured patients, preventing frivolous lawsuits, or discouraging negligence. The remedies for these shortcomings are not obvious. A dynamic marketplace that allows parties to experiment with—and abandon—different malpractice rules is the quickest and surest way to arrive at those solutions.

9. HEALTH INSURANCE REGULATION

State legislators should

- eliminate government licensing of health insurance;
- or, as preliminary steps, recognize insurance licenses from other states and U.S. territories;
- remove all restrictions on short-term, limited-duration health insurance; and
- remove Farm Bureau plans and direct primary care from the purview of state insurance regulators.

Congress should

- repeal the Patient Protection and Affordable Care Act (ACA, or Obamacare) and other federal laws restricting health insurance choice;
- eliminate states' ability to use licensing laws to prevent residents from purchasing insurance from out-of-state insurers; and
- relinquish any role as an insurance regulator.

Regulation Blocks Reliable Health Insurance

Federal and state governments impose countless regulations that increase health insurance premiums, reduce the quality of coverage for all consumers, and limit the right of consumers to purchase the health insurance plans of their choice.

Worse, the Patient Protection and Affordable Care Act's supposed "protections" for preexisting conditions *cause* discrimination against the sick. Such discrimination "completely undermines the goal of the ACA."[1] Regulation-induced discrimination against the sick is so extensive, even "currently healthy consumers cannot be adequately insured against . . . one of the poorly covered chronic disease[s]."[2]

Congress can and should make health insurance better, more affordable, and more secure by repealing Obamacare and other federal health insurance regulations. States likewise should eliminate state-level health insurance regulations. At the very least, states should free their residents to purchase insurance from states and U.S. territories with more consumer-friendly regulations.

Community Rating: High Premiums, Junk Coverage

The heart of Obamacare's supposed protections for patients with preexisting conditions is a requirement that insurers offer coverage to all applicants ("guaranteed issue") and price controls on the premiums that insurers can charge ("community rating"). Guaranteed issue requires insurers to offer coverage even to applicants with preexisting medical conditions that by definition are uninsurable.

Community rating limits insurers' ability to set premiums according to the health risk of individual enrollees. Obamacare requires insurers to cover all comers and to charge all enrollees of a given age the same premium, regardless of health status. Insurers may charge older enrollees no more than three times the youngest enrollees, even though the oldest typically cost six or seven times more. Community rating reduces premiums for enrollees with preexisting conditions at the cost of higher premiums and worse health insurance for everyone including many sick patients.

Obamacare's community-rating price controls are the driving force behind the law's rising premiums.[3] Under Obamacare, premiums in the individual market doubled in four years, an average annual increase of 20 percent.[4] One fourth of Obamacare plans have submitted premium increases of 10 percent or more for 2024.[5] According to the *Washington Post*, women ages 55–64 saw the largest premium increases:

> Total expected premiums and out of pocket expenses rose [in 2014] by 50 percent for women age 55 to 64—a much larger increase than for any other group—for policies on the federal exchanges relative to prices that individuals who bought individual insurance before health care reform went into effect. . . . Premiums for the second-lowest silver policy are 67 percent higher for a 55 to 64-year-old woman than they were pre-ACA.[6]

By 2021, Congress was offering taxpayer subsidies of $12,000 to people earning $212,000 a year just to help them afford Obamacare premiums.[7]

Though the purpose of community rating is to make health insurance available to those who have never had health insurance or who lost it before they got sick, an unintended consequence is that it makes health insurance worse for everyone, including many sick patients who purchased coverage before they got sick. Community rating degrades health insurance quality in several ways.

First, 83 percent of consumers value the freedom to choose when their coverage begins.[8] Markets make this possible by allowing consumers to enroll and switch plans throughout the year. Community rating denies consumers this right by requiring insurers to sell coverage only during specific, brief periods. Consumers may not purchase coverage outside those "open" or "special" enrollment periods.[9] ObamaCare's community-rating price controls thus deny sick and healthy consumers alike the right to enroll in coverage for 9–10 months of the year. In many cases, it denies consumers coverage when they need it most.

Second, community rating penalizes high-quality coverage. Obamacare's community-rating price controls penalize insurers if they offer high-quality coverage that attracts patients with nerve pain (penalty: $3,000 per patient), severe acne ($4,000 per patient), diabetes insipidus or hemophilia A ($5,000 per patient), substance abuse disorder ($6,000 per patient), multiple sclerosis ($14,000 per patient), infertility ($15,000 per patient), or other conditions.[10]

The insurers who suffer those penalties are those that offer *better* coverage for the sick than their competitors. Community rating therefore forces insurers to eliminate health plans and plan features that sick people value to ensure that they provide worse coverage for the sick than their competitors. It even rewards insurers if they unintentionally make coverage worse for the sick, such as by not updating provider networks.[11] If insurers fail to engage in such "backdoor discrimination," community rating threatens them with insolvency.[12]

The result is a race to the bottom. Researchers have shown that community rating eliminated comprehensive health plans for employees of Harvard University, Stanford University, the Massachusetts Institute of Technology, the state of Minnesota, and the federal government.[13] In Obamacare, patient advocacy groups have identified backdoor discrimination against patients with cancer, cystic fibrosis, hepatitis, HIV, and other illnesses. Community rating generates "poor coverage for the medications demanded by [sick] patients," restricts patients' choice of doctors and hospitals, and rewards other plan features that make coverage worse for the sick.[14]

Community rating's race to the bottom "undoes intended protections for preexisting conditions," creates a marketplace where even "currently healthy consumers cannot be adequately insured," and "completely undermines the goal of the ACA."[15] Community rating replaces a form of discrimination that affects *few* patients with an arguably worse form of discrimination that harms *all* patients.

Community rating increases the incentives insurers face to renege on their commitments to the sick. Prior to Obamacare, innovations like guaranteed renewability enabled insurers to profit by building up reserves to provide quality coverage for enrollees who became ill. Community rating led insurers to give those reserves away to healthy people.[16]

Finally, community rating can ultimately cause health insurance markets to collapse, leaving consumers with no way to afford medical care. It has caused the total or partial collapse, for example, of health insurance markets in California, Kentucky, Maine, Massachusetts, New Hampshire, New Jersey, New York, Vermont, and Washington.[17]

Obamacare's community-rating price controls caused markets for child-only health insurance to collapse totally in 17 states and partially in 22 states.[18] Obamacare's community-rated long-term-care insurance program collapsed before launch. The Obama administration exempted U.S. territories from community rating lest those markets collapse as well. The only thing keeping Obamacare from completely collapsing under the weight of community rating is $91 billion in annual taxpayer subsidies, including subsidies of $12,000 for people earning $212,000 a year.[19]

Community Rating Blocks Affordable, Secure, Quality Coverage

Community rating has destroyed innovative insurance products and prevented the development of further innovations that provide secure coverage to people who develop preexisting conditions.

Guaranteed-renewable health insurance is an innovation that allows consumers who develop expensive conditions to keep purchasing coverage at healthy-person premiums. Prior to Obamacare, even though insurers could deny coverage or charge higher premiums to those with preexisting conditions, consumers in poor health with guaranteed renewable coverage were less likely to lose their coverage and end up uninsured than consumers in poor health who had employer-sponsored coverage (see Figure 9.1). Insurers built up reserves to cover those costs. When Obamacare imposed community rating, it made guaranteed-renewable health insurance impossible and transferred resources away from the sick. Blue Cross and Blue Shield of North Carolina, for example, had accumulated a $156 million guaranteed-renewability reserve fund to cover its sickest enrollees. Community rating led the insurer to return that money to policyholders as refunds averaging $725 each—that is, to take money that markets had set aside for the sick and give it away to the healthy.

Obamacare destroyed another innovation that markets had just begun to introduce. In 2008 and 2009, insurance regulators in 25 states approved the sale of "preexisting-conditions insurance." These products protected workers

Figure 9.1
Guaranteed renewability makes individual-market coverage more secure than employer coverage, 2000–2004

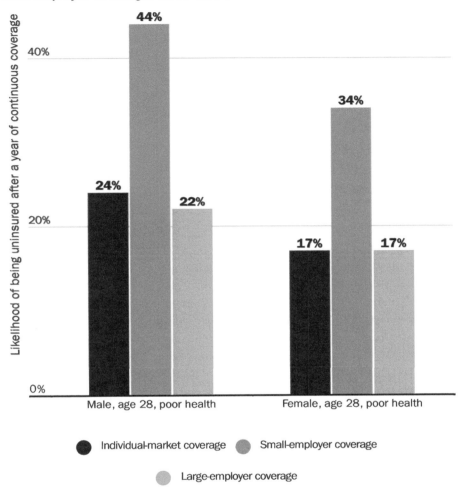

Source: Mark V. Pauly and Robert D. Lieberthal, "How Risky Is Individual Health Insurance?," *Health Affairs* 27, no. 1 (2008).
Note: Assumes family income of $50,000 annually, expecting a 4 percent increase in income.

with employer-sponsored health insurance against higher premiums if they transitioned to an individual-market plan after falling ill. Like guaranteed renewability, preexisting-conditions insurance allowed those who developed an expensive, long-term medical condition to keep paying healthy-person premiums. UnitedHealthcare offered this revolutionary product for 20 percent of the cost of the underlying individual-market policy.

Community rating is blocking additional innovations. Two examples illustrate the possibilities. Law professors Peter Siegelman and Tom Baker explain how insurers could make health insurance more attractive to so-called young invincibles, and induce them to purchase it voluntarily, by offering cash rebates to people who don't file claims.[20] Economist John Cochrane explains how insurers could offer total satisfaction guarantees.[21] Insurance contracts could allow sick enrollees who grow dissatisfied with their coverage to fire their insurance company, receive a large cash payout, and then choose from among other carriers who would compete to cover them. Markets protect the sick from incentives that insurers face to renege on their commitments. Obamacare increases those incentives.

For all the damage guaranteed-issue and community-rating regulations cause, they appear to offer little benefit when it comes to expanding coverage to the sick. After comparing community rating to unregulated markets before Obamacare imposed community rating in all states, economist Mark Pauly and his colleagues concluded:

> We find that [community rating] modestly tempers the (already small) relationship of premium to risk, and leads to a slight increase in the *relative* probability that high-risk people will obtain individual coverage. However, we also find that the increase in overall premiums from community rating slightly reduces the total number of people buying insurance. All of the effects of regulation are quite small, though. We conjecture that the reason for the minimal impact is that guaranteed renewability already accomplishes a large part of effective risk averaging (without the regulatory burden), so additional regulation has little left to change.[22]

If Obamacare has expanded coverage, its vast subsidies for insurance companies are the reason, not community rating.

Additional Harmful Regulations

State and federal governments have enacted additional health insurance regulations that harm patients.

"Any-willing-provider" laws increase prices for medical care and health insurance premiums. Insurers frequently negotiate discounts from providers. In exchange, they steer enrollees toward those providers. More than half the states have enacted any-willing-provider laws, which require insurers to offer the same payment levels to all providers.[23] "Any-willing-provider legislation removes the incentive to compete aggressively on a price basis," writes health economist Michael Morrisey. "No one has an incentive to offer much of a discount since discounts will result only in lower prices with little or no expanded volume."[24] The results are higher prices for medical care and higher health insurance premiums.

State and federal governments also make health insurance less affordable by requiring consumers to purchase coverage they do not want. Many states require consumers to purchase coverage for services that some may consider quackery, such as acupuncture, chiropractic, and naturopathy. Thirty-three states require consumers to purchase at least 40 types of mandated coverage.[25] States have also required consumers to purchase coverage for medical treatments that later proved harmful to health, such as high-dose chemotherapy with autologous bone marrow transplant for breast cancer.[26]

States impose many additional regulations on insurance pools, from premium taxes to rules that reduce insurers' ability to limit fraud and wasteful services. The nonpartisan Congressional Budget Office has estimated that, on average, state health insurance regulations increase premiums by 13 percent.[27] States then prevent individuals and employers from avoiding unwanted regulatory costs by prohibiting them from purchasing health insurance from jurisdictions with more consumer-friendly regulations.

Repeal Obamacare

Congress should repeal Obamacare and replace it with reforms that allow better, more affordable, and more secure health insurance. Premiums would fall for millions of Americans who would no longer have to buy coverage they do not want or pay hidden taxes that further increase their premiums. Consumers could purchase coverage that is more secure than either Obamacare coverage or employer-sponsored insurance. They would have the option to purchase preexisting-conditions insurance, which would provide protection from the financial costs of long-term illness at a fraction of the cost of a standard health insurance plan. Consumers could look forward to the day when health insurance comes with total-satisfaction guarantees that force insurers to compete aggressively on quality.

Merely repealing Obamacare is not enough to improve quality and expand access for those currently receiving subsidies under its auspices. Federal and state policymakers must take additional steps to achieve that goal (see the remainder of this chapter plus Chapters 5–8 and 10–12).

As Congress takes these steps to transition the U.S. health care sector from a government-run system to a market system, political necessity may require Congress to offer transitional assistance to the relatively small number who receive coverage under Obamacare but would not see their premiums fall after repeal. The block grants that Chapter 12 recommends could provide such assistance. If repealing Obamacare is politically infeasible at the moment, state and federal lawmakers can allow alternatives to free consumers from Obamacare's junk coverage. Alternative coverage options can coexist alongside Obamacare, reduce its premiums by giving sicker patients a better alternative, and provide a benchmark against which to measure Obamacare's performance.[28]

Congress already exempts certain health plans from Obamacare's harmful regulations. Federal law has exempted "short-term, limited-duration" insurance (STLDI) from nearly all federal regulation for decades. Such plans often cost 70 percent less than Obamacare plans and offer a broader choice of doctors and hospitals.[29] In 2018, federal regulators clarified that the exemption is broad enough that insurers can pair these plans with renewal guarantees to provide secure, long-term coverage.[30] (A better descriptor of such plans is renewable term health insurance.[31]) Congress should encourage insurers to enter the market and prevent future regulators from later denying consumers these choices by codifying that interpretation. States should likewise exempt such plans from their own regulations and give consumers full flexibility to take advantage of these plans.[32] Specifically, states should let consumers (1) purchase STLDI with an initial term of up to 12 months, (2) renew the initial STLDI contract for up to 36 months, and (3) purchase stand-alone "renewal guarantees" that protect them from reunderwriting in perpetuity.

The Obama administration allowed another alternative to Obamacare. In 2014, it ruled that Obamacare's most expensive regulations—"guaranteed availability, community rating, single risk pool, rate review, medical loss ratio and essential health benefits"—do not apply in U.S. territories.[33] States can and should make health insurance better, more affordable, and more secure by allowing their residents (including employers) to purchase health plans available in American Samoa, Guam, the Northern Marianas Islands, Puerto Rico, or the U.S. Virgin Islands.[34] Major insurers with networks in the 50 states —including Aetna, UnitedHealthcare, Humana, and Blue Cross Blue Shield —already do business in the territories. Restoring the right of state residents to purchase such plans would also provide an economic boost to struggling territories.

Several states allow associations of farmers (Farm Bureaus) to offer health insurance free from costly state regulations.[35] Farm Bureau coverage presents another opportunity for insurers to offer lower-cost plans that provide secure coverage through innovations such as renewal guarantees, and that can therefore improve Obamacare risk pools and reduce Obamacare premiums. All states should allow Farm Bureaus and other associations to offer such coverage.

State insurance regulators often inhibit entry by defining innovations in health care delivery as insurance, and thus subjecting them to onerous and inappropriate regulation. "Direct primary care" (DPC) allows consumers to get quicker access to primary care by paying a monthly or yearly subscription fee. Because DPC involves some pooling of medical expenses, regulators often define it as insurance. Dozens of states have enacted laws putting DPC outside the reach of insurance regulators. All states should do so.

Repeal State Insurance-Licensing Laws

State insurance-licensing laws give each state's insurance regulators a monopoly over providing consumer protections to insurance purchasers. Regulators then do what all monopolists do: provide a low-quality product at an excessive cost.

The best solution is for states to repeal insurance-licensing laws. Full liberalization would maximize quality, affordability, and innovation. It would eliminate government's ability to use insurance regulations to redistribute income, or to shower rents on favored special interests. Competition and government enforcement of contracts would continue to provide the financial solvency protections and other safeguards that insurance purchasers demand.

If repealing insurance-licensing laws is politically infeasible, preliminary steps could provide nearly as much benefit to consumers.[36] Under one approach, the federal or state governments could allow individuals and employers to purchase health insurance licensed by other states. If purchasers are content with their own state's consumer protections, they could continue to purchase a policy their state licenses. If their state imposes too many mandates, or prevents insurance pools from protecting participants from irresponsible or opportunistic behavior, they could choose an insurance plan from a state with more consumer-friendly regulations.

"Regulatory federalism" would increase competition in health insurance markets. Insurers would face lower barriers to introducing products into new states. As a result, consumers would have much greater choice among cost-saving features (e.g., cost sharing and care management), provider financial incentives (fee-for-service, prepayment, and hybrids of the two), and delivery systems (integrated, nonintegrated, and everything in between). (See Chapter 5.) Insurance pools would be more stable, and consumers would have more freedom to obtain coverage that fits their needs.

Perhaps most important, regulatory federalism would force insurance *regulators* to compete with one another to provide the optimal level of regulation. States that impose unwanted regulatory costs on insurance purchasers would see their residents' business—and their premium tax revenue—go elsewhere.

The desire to retain premium tax revenue would drive states to eliminate unwanted, costly regulations and retain only those regulations that consumers value. One or a handful of states would likely emerge as the dominant regulators in a national marketplace, just as Delaware created a niche for itself by offering a hospitable regulatory environment for corporate chartering, and South Dakota did with credit card operations.[37]

A Race to Consumer Satisfaction

Some critics claim that letting individuals and employers purchase coverage from other states would lead to a race to the bottom as states eager to attract premium tax revenue would eliminate all regulatory protections or skimp on enforcement. On the contrary, it is regulatory monopolies and specific regulations like community rating that create a race to the bottom. Competition *prevents* a race to the bottom. As producers of consumer protections, states are unlikely to attract or retain premium-tax revenue by offering an inferior product. Consumers and ultimately insurers would avoid states whose regulations prove inadequate. Moreover, the first people to suffer from insufficient consumer protections would be residents of that state, who would then demand that their legislators enact better consumer protections. Regulatory federalism would not produce a race to the bottom but a race to consumer satisfaction where states only adopt consumer protections whose benefits justify the costs.

To enforce consumer protections, states could require out-of-state insurers to incorporate the licensing state's regulations into the insurance contract. That way, consumers could enforce those regulations in their own state, rather than in the state that licensed the insurance policy. Such "choice-of-law" decisions are complex but rest on extensive legal doctrine and precedent. A state's insurance regulators could even play a role in policing and enforcing other states' regulatory protections.

Ideally, each state would unilaterally give its residents the right to purchase insurance from any other state. All that each state and territory need do is deem insurance policies that hold licenses from other states or territories as being in compliance with that state's laws.

A surer approach might be for Congress to act. The U.S. Constitution grants Congress the power to regulate commerce among the states largely to prevent states from erecting trade barriers that keep out products from other states. Insurance-licensing laws are a clear example of such trade barriers. Congress need not alter any state's health insurance regulations. All that is necessary is for Congress to require states and territories to recognize the insurance licenses from other states and territories.

However, the Constitution does not grant Congress the power to regulate health insurance, so the same legislation should relinquish any role for Congress as an insurance regulator. Were Congress to assume that role, it would become a monopoly provider of consumer protections. The result would be high-cost, low-quality coverage that is far more difficult to dislodge than state regulation.

Any federal law aimed at regulatory federalism must do nothing more than allow consumers to purchase health insurance regulated by another state and ensure that those are the only regulations that govern. If Congress uses the opportunity to regulate health insurance itself, reform will not have been worth the effort.

10. THE TAX TREATMENT OF HEALTH CARE

State legislators should

- avoid creating any preferential tax treatment for health insurance or medical care; and
- eliminate existing tax preferences for health insurance and medical care while reducing the overall tax burden.

Congress should

- avoid creating health insurance tax credits or any other preferential tax treatment for health insurance or medical care;
- replace all existing health-related tax preferences with an income- and payroll-tax exclusion for "large" health savings accounts; and subsequently
- adopt a new tax system that reduces tax rates by eliminating all tax preferences for particular forms of consumption.

One of the most far-reaching and damaging ways that government intervenes in the health sector of the economy is through the tax system. The U.S. government taxes incomes and payrolls. Many state governments tax incomes. In each case, governments exempt certain health-related uses of income from taxation. Treating health and nonhealth consumption differently under the tax code effectively penalizes taxpayers who do not spend their money on the health care goods and services the tax code favors. State and federal policymakers should eliminate all such targeted tax preferences, which have done enormous harm to consumers and patients. If government must tax incomes, it should tax all income equally.

The imperative of eliminating targeted tax preferences has bedeviled policymakers for decades. The best politically feasible option is to expand tax-free health savings accounts (HSAs).

The Tax Exclusion for Employer-Sponsored Health Insurance

By far the largest of these tax preferences is the exclusion from the federal income and payroll tax bases of employer-sponsored health insurance benefits. Workers who receive income from an employer in the form of health insurance pay no income or payroll tax on the money the employer pays toward the premium. Federal and state governments exclude that spending from the income and payroll tax bases. Under so-called Section 125 plans, many workers pay no tax on the portion of the premium they pay, either.

As a result of the tax exclusion for employer-sponsored health insurance, federal and state tax codes effectively penalize workers who choose not to enroll in employer-sponsored health insurance. Workers who do not enroll in such plans pay higher taxes than workers who do. If two jobs offer equivalent total compensation but one offers health coverage and the other offers higher cash wages, the tax code effectively penalizes the worker who chooses the job that offers higher cash wages. In 2021, the average annual premium for employer-sponsored family coverage was $22,221 (of which the employer paid $16,253 and the worker paid $5,969).[1] Assuming a marginal tax rate of 33 percent, the tax code effectively penalized the worker $7,333 for taking the second job. The additional income and payroll taxes the worker must pay are the functional equivalent of a penalty for making the "wrong" choice.

Economy-wide, employers and workers spent $1.3 trillion on employee health benefits in 2022. Employers paid $944 billion on their workers' behalf; workers paid $327 billion directly. If all workers had decided to decline their health benefits, they would have retained that $327 billion and a competitive labor market would have returned the remaining $944 billion to them. The tax code would then have treated all $1.3 trillion as taxable income and forced workers to pay roughly an additional $352 billion in taxes—effectively penalizing workers for not allowing their employers to control $1.3 trillion of their earnings and their health insurance decisions.

Policymakers and scholars describe the exclusion as a tax break. It is more accurate and useful to recognize that it turns income and payroll taxes into an implicit penalty on workers who do not (a) surrender control of a sizable portion of their earnings to an employer; (b) enroll in a health plan that their employers choose, control, and revoke upon separation; and (c) pay the balance of the premium directly. Those implicit penalties collectively deny workers control of $1 trillion of their earnings per year.

The tax exclusion for employer-sponsored health insurance is the largest source of compulsory spending in the United States, larger than the federal Medicare program (see Figure 10.1). It is the principal reason why the United

Figure 10.1
Employer-sponsored health insurance is the largest source of compulsory health spending in the United States, 2022

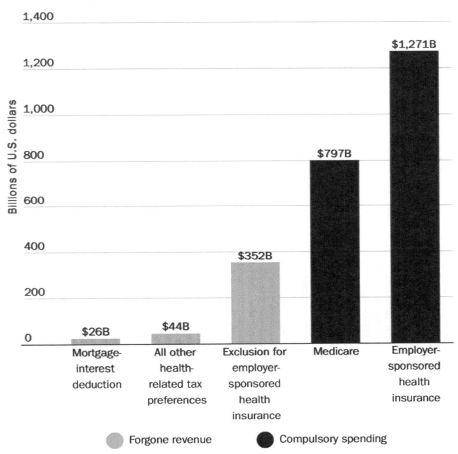

Source: U.S. Office of Management and Budget, "Tax Expenditures," in *Analytical Perspectives: Budget of the U.S. Government, Fiscal Year 2022* (Washington: Government Publishing Office, 2021), pp. 111, 113; "The Budget and Economic Outlook: 2021 to 2031," Congressional Budget Office, February 2021, p. 5; Boards of Trustees, "2021 Annual Report of the Boards of Trustees of the Federal Hospital Insurance and Federal Supplementary Medical Insurance Trust Funds," Federal Hospital Insurance and Federal Supplementary Medical Insurance Trust Funds, August 31, 2021, p. 111; National Health Statistics Group, "Table 5-6—Private Health Insurance by Sponsor: Calendar Years 1987–2020," Office of the Actuary, Centers for Medicare & Medicaid Services, Department of Health and Human Services; National Health Statistics Group, "Table 16—National Health Expenditures (NHE), Amounts and Average Growth Annual Growth from Previous Year Shown, by Type or Sponsor, Selected Calendar Years 2011–2028," Office of the Actuary, Centers for Medicare & Medicaid Services, Department of Health and Human Services; and author's calculations.

Figure 10.2

Government compels U.S. residents to spend a larger share of GDP on health care than residents of other OECD nations, 2020

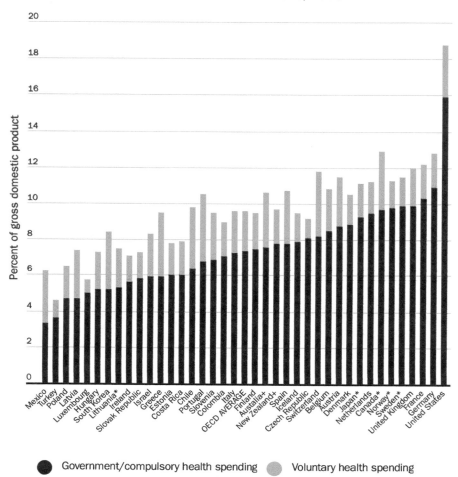

Government/compulsory health spending ● ● Voluntary health spending

Source: "Health spending Total/Government/compulsory, % of GDP, 2020," Organisation for Economic Co-operation and Development, https://data.oecd.org/chart/6Lr9.
Note: GDP = gross domestic product; OECD = Organisation for Economic Co-operation and Development; * = provisional data; + = estimated data.

States ranks far and away the highest among advanced nations in compulsory health spending as a share of GDP (see Figure 10.2) and eighth highest among advanced nations in compulsory health spending as a share of total health spending (see Figure 10.3). It is why 56 percent of the U.S. population obtains health insurance through an employer and only 10 percent obtain it directly from an insurance company.

Figure 10.3
Compulsory spending comprises a larger share of health spending in the United States than in most other OECD nations, 2020

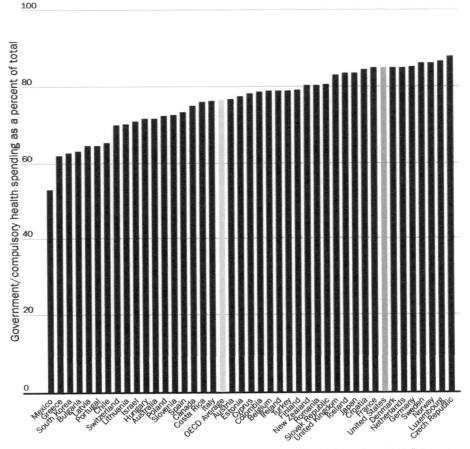

Source: "Health spending Total/Government/Compulsory, % of Health Spending, 2020," Organisation for Economic Co-operation and Development, https://data.oecd.org/chart/6LrL.
Note: OECD = Organisation for Economic Co-operation and Development.

Harms of the Tax Exclusion

The exclusion does enormous harm to consumers and patients. It generates excessive medical prices and health insurance premiums. It strips coverage from people with preexisting conditions, leaving them with nothing. It restricts consumer choice: 80 percent of covered workers have only one or two plan types from which to choose. It inhibits wage growth and improvements in health care quality. It makes workers more vulnerable to public-health crises. It reduces economic productivity on the order of 1 percent of GDP each year.

The exclusion leaves many workers who should and could have had secure health insurance coverage with uninsured and uninsurable preexisting conditions. The average worker changes jobs a dozen times by age 52.[2] Health insurance that consumers purchase directly from an insurance company covers the policyholder between jobs and into retirement. In 1964, "many Americans over sixty-five were covered by health insurance policies that were guaranteed renewable for life" because more than 70 insurance companies offered such coverage.[3]

The exclusion penalizes workers unless they enroll in health insurance that automatically disappears when they quit their job, lose their job, keep their job but lose their benefits, lose a spouse to divorce or death, age off a parent's plan, retire, or become too sick to work. The exclusion thus strips millions of workers of their coverage after they develop an expensive medical condition. Workers in poor health are roughly twice as likely to end up with no insurance if they obtained coverage from a small employer versus purchasing it themselves (see Figure 10.4). In 1964, the elderly had lower rates of health insurance than the overall population. A principal reason was "many . . . who had insurance coverage before retirement were unable to retain the coverage after retirement . . . because the policy was available to employed persons only."[4] For decades, the tax code has literally penalized workers who choose more-secure health insurance.

Economists Martin Feldstein and Bernard Friedman write, "It can with justice be said that the tax [exclusion] has been responsible for much of the health care crisis."[5]

One Mistake That Launched Hundreds More

The exclusion has prompted Congress to intervene in the health sector again and again to mitigate its harmful effects.

- In 1965, Congress created Medicare largely to help seniors whom the exclusion stripped of their insurance. Since Congress based Medicare coverage on the (excessive) coverage employers offered, the exclusion indirectly increased the cost of Medicare. (Meanwhile, Medicare's ever-rising payroll tax increased the exclusion's impact by increasing its implicit penalties.)
- Also in 1965, Congress created Medicaid to help patients who could not afford the excessive prices that were the result of the exclusion.

Figure 10.4
For enrollees in poor health, individual-market coverage is more secure than employer coverage, 2000–2004

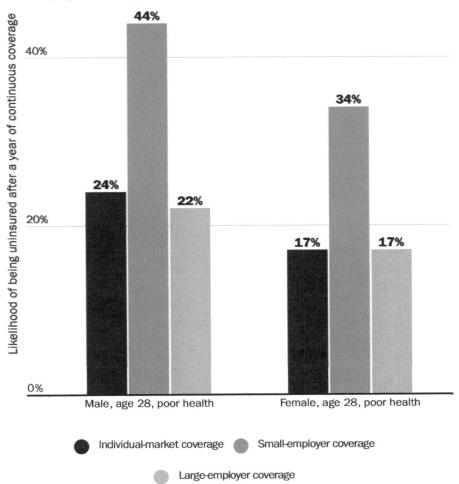

Source: Mark V. Pauly and Robert D. Lieberthal, "How Risky Is Individual Health Insurance?," *Health Affairs* 27, no. 1 (2008).
Note: Assumes family income of $50,000 annually, expecting a 4 percent increase in income.

- In 1973, Congress passed the Health Maintenance Organization (HMO) Act to subsidize and require certain employers to offer health plans that the exclusion discourages.
- In 1974, Congress enacted the National Health Planning and Resources Development Act, which encouraged states to enact "certificate of need"

laws (see Chapter 6) to curb the excessive health spending that results from the exclusion.

- In 1978, Congress made employee payments toward employer-plan premiums eligible for the exclusion—thereby trying to make health insurance affordable by expanding a policy that makes it more expensive.
- In 1985, Congress enacted the Consolidated Omnibus Budget Reconciliation Act (COBRA) to aid workers whom the exclusion strips of their coverage.
- In 1996, Congress enacted the Health Insurance Portability and Accountability Act (HIPAA) to help those who lose the coverage the exclusion forced them to take.
- In 1997, Congress created the Children's Health Insurance Program (CHIP) to aid families for whom the exclusion made coverage too expensive.
- In 2009, Congress enacted the Health Information Technology for Economic and Clinical Health (HITECH) Act to encourage electronic medical records, which the exclusion discourages.
- In 2010, Congress passed the Patient Protection and Affordable Care Act (Obamacare) to aid patients whom the exclusion strips of coverage and leaves with uninsurable preexisting conditions.
- In 2020, Congress passed the No Surprises Act to discourage surprise medical bills, which the exclusion encourages.

Since creating Medicare, Medicaid, CHIP, and Obamacare, Congress has continuously expanded each of these programs to aid those who cannot afford health insurance or medical care at the excessive prices the exclusion generates. Federal antitrust authorities have repeatedly taken action against market consolidation that the exclusion encourages.[6] Congress has enacted countless other pieces of legislation to counteract the exclusion's cost-increasing and quality-suppressing effects. Rather than resolve the situation, each of these efforts has made the exclusion's underlying problems worse.

Congress has also expanded the exclusion with various spending or savings vehicles that allow workers to purchase medical care tax-free. One of those vehicles—tax-free HSAs—creates an opportunity to return to workers control of the $1 trillion of their earnings that the exclusion denies them.

Reforming the Tax Exclusion with Large HSAs

Individuals have a right to choose for themselves whether, where, and how much health insurance and medical care to purchase, without government penalizing them. The tax system should offer no special tax breaks or penalties for health-related expenditures or any other type of consumption.

The best way to eliminate tax-based distortions of workers' health care decisions is to eliminate income and payroll taxes, which have done enormous harm to workers. Barring that, federal lawmakers should eliminate the exclusion for employer-sponsored insurance and other health-related tax preferences. Unfortunately, those options do not appear politically feasible at present. The repeal of the "Cadillac tax," which would have merely limited the exclusion, suggests workers will resist reforms that do nothing but eliminate health-related tax breaks. Rather, the best politically feasible way to reform the tax treatment of health care is by changing the current exclusion into an exclusion for larger, more flexible HSAs.

HSAs enable workers to save money for their health care expenses tax-free. At present, employer contributions to a worker's HSA enjoy the same tax-free status as employer-paid insurance premiums. As a result, workers do not have to surrender those earnings to their employer to avoid the exclusion's implicit penalties. Taxpayers can also make tax-preferred contributions themselves. Account holders can use HSA funds to purchase qualified medical expenses, tax-free, from any source. HSA funds belong to the individual, follow the individual from job to job, and grow tax-free.

Still, HSAs enable workers to control only a small portion of the dollars and decisions that tax laws allow employers to control. HSAs create tax parity only for the funds that account holders contribute to the HSA to cover out-of-pocket medical expenses. If workers want to purchase their own health insurance, generally they must still pay the premiums with after-tax dollars. Only consumers with insurance that meets Congress's rigid definition of a "qualified high-deductible health plan" can make tax-free HSA deposits. HSAs are small comfort to workers whose employer doesn't offer them, or who dislike the one narrow type of health plan Congress permits HSA holders to obtain.

Nevertheless, HSAs present an opportunity to enact reforms that would make health care better, more affordable, and more secure. Congress should take these steps to expand HSAs:

- eliminate all other health-related tax preferences;
- apply the tax exclusion for employer-sponsored health insurance solely to funds that individuals or employers contribute to an HSA;
- increase HSA contribution limits dramatically, from $3,650 for individuals and $7,300 for families to (say) $9,000 for individuals and $18,000 for families;
- remove the requirement that HSA holders obtain a qualified high-deductible health plan, or any health plan; and

- allow HSA holders to purchase health insurance, of any type and from any source, tax-free with HSA funds.

Replacing all existing health-related tax preferences with one tax break for "large" HSAs would limit the exclusion and all tax-based distortions of the health sector. It would free workers to choose their doctor and their health plans without penalty.

Large HSAs would minimize political resistance to reform. First, rather than increase taxes as the Cadillac tax did, large HSAs would give all workers an effective tax cut. Even if large HSAs were revenue neutral, and even though some workers (whose prior health benefits spending exceeded the higher contribution limits) would face a higher explicit tax liability, nearly all workers would receive an effective tax cut because they would get to control a large portion of their income that their employer currently controls. Workers with family coverage would gain control of an average $16,253 that they currently do not control. That effective tax cut would swamp any additional tax liability that some workers might pay. Economy-wide, large HSAs would allow workers to gain control of $1 trillion of their earnings each year. Large HSAs are the only reform that includes a mechanism to return those earnings to workers immediately. They would return to workers a larger share of GDP than even the Reagan tax cuts of 1981 (see Figure 10.5). Second, workers and employers who like their current health insurance arrangements could keep them.

Large HSAs would reduce barriers to innovative insurance products. Workers could choose any health plan they like and would become cost-conscious when shopping for insurance in a way they have never been. This dynamic would eliminate the tax code's barriers to prepaid group plans and thereby bring innovations like comparative-effectiveness research, electronic medical records, and coordinated care within the reach of hundreds of millions of Americans. The change would drive down prices by encouraging the growth of retail clinics and removing barriers to reverse deductibles, which have saved consumers thousands of dollars on medical procedures (see Figure 10.6). Large HSAs could change the politics of health care by making consumers more conscious of the costs of government regulation.

Endgame: Tax Neutrality for Health Care

Large HSAs would facilitate the transition to a tax system that contains no special preferences—exclusions, deductions, exemptions, or credits—for health care or any other form of consumption. They would allow such fundamental tax reform to proceed in two steps. First, they would give workers immediate control of the $1 trillion that employers now spend on their workers' behalf.

Figure 10.5
Expanding health savings accounts would return a larger share of GDP to workers than past tax cuts

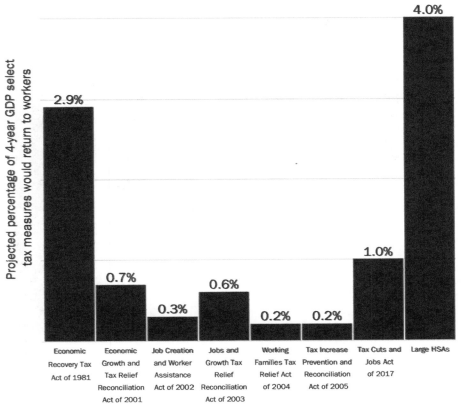

Source: Jerry Tempalski, "Revenue Effects of Major Tax Bills, Updated Tables for all 2012 Bills," Office of Tax Analysis, Department of the Treasury, February 2013; National Health Statistics Group, "Table 5-6—Private Health Insurance by Sponsor: Calendar Years 1987–2020," Office of the Actuary, Centers for Medicare & Medicaid Services, Department of Health and Human Services; National Health Statistics Group, "Table 16—National Health Expenditures (NHE), Amounts and Average Annual Growth from Previous Year Shown, by Type or Sponsor, Selected Calendar Years 2011–2028," Office of the Actuary, Centers for Medicare & Medicaid Services, Department of Health and Human Services; Congressional Budget Office, "Re: Cost Estimate for the Conference Agreement on H.R. 1, a Bill to Provide for Reconciliation Pursuant to Titles II and V of the Concurrent Resolution on the Budget for Fiscal Year 2018," letter to Kevin Brady (chairman of the House Committee on Ways and Means), December 15, 2017; Office of Management and Budget, "Historical Tables, Budget of the United States Government, Fiscal Year 2019," February 12, 2018, p. 27; and author's calculations.
Notes: GDP = gross domestic product; HSA = health savings account.

Figure 10.6
Price-conscious patients lower prices: Average price reductions within two years of patients becoming price-conscious

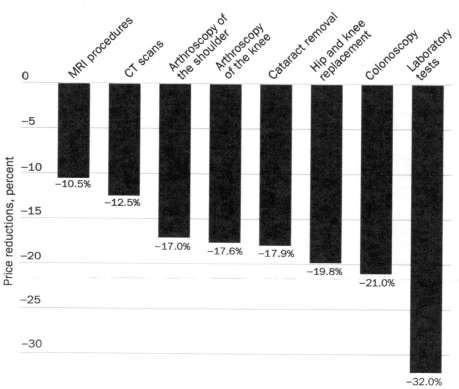

Source: James Robinson, Timothy Brown, and Cristopher Whaley, "Reference Pricing Changes the 'Choice Architecture' of Health Care for Consumers," *Health Affairs* 36, no. 3 (March 2017): 524–30.

All other reforms of the exclusion create uncertainty about what will become of those funds. Large HSAs eliminate that uncertainty by immediately delivering those funds to workers. Second, once workers control those funds, Congress could enact fundamental reform without the obstacle of consumers' anxieties about whether they will be able to keep their health insurance or whether employers will return to them what is rightfully theirs. With large HSAs, it would be far easier for Congress to transition to a flat, fair, or national sales tax.

The tax exclusion for employer-sponsored health insurance is why the United States does not have, and never has had, a private or voluntary or market-based health insurance system. The United States will not have a consumer-centered health sector until workers control the $1.3 trillion of their earnings that the exclusion now lets employers control.

Congress should act immediately to eliminate the exclusion. At a minimum, it should reduce the harms that the exclusion causes by taking serious steps to reform it. Replacing the exclusion with large HSAs is the best politically feasible option.

11. MEDICARE

Congress should

- phase out Medicare in favor of a better system as rapidly as possible;
- take every opportunity to cut Medicare spending;
- give Medicare's entire budget directly to enrollees as cash ("Medicare checks");
- give higher payments to enrollees with lower lifetime incomes and higher disease burdens, in a budget-neutral manner;
- eliminate quality-suppressing regulations (e.g., community-rating price controls) and regulations that favor particular levels or types of health insurance for Medicare enrollees;
- limit the growth of Medicare spending to gross domestic product growth (at most);
- allow current workers to save their Medicare payroll taxes in personal, inheritable accounts that would gradually replace Medicare checks; and
- fund any transition costs by reducing other government spending.

Since 1965, the U.S. Medicare program has denied workers the right to decide whether and how to spend their money on medical care. It has increased prices for medical care and health insurance, including for nonenrollees, and has reduced health care quality.

Congress finances Medicare spending by taxing younger workers. The program currently spends roughly $1 trillion per year to subsidize health care for 64 million enrollees who are elderly, are disabled, or who meet other criteria.[1] In dollar terms, Medicare is the largest purchaser of medical care goods and services in the world—in part because it pays excessive prices to health care providers and wastes hundreds of billions of dollars on medical care that provides no value to enrollees.[2]

Perhaps worst of all, Medicare is junk insurance. For more than 50 years, Medicare has had a negative impact on the quality of health care that both enrollees and nonenrollees receive. When researchers complain about fee-for-service payment, wasteful care, low-quality care, harmful care, medical errors, health care fraud, excessive profits, high administrative costs, federal deficits and debt, the time bomb of entitlement spending, special-interest influence over health care, or the lack of innovation in health care delivery, evidence-based medicine, electronic medical records, accountable care organizations, telemedicine, or coordinated care—in every case they are complaining about Medicare.

Though neither Republicans nor Democrats like to admit it, Medicare is already a voucher program that allows enrollees to choose to receive their subsidy either through a government-run "public option" (traditional Medicare) or private insurers (Medicare Advantage).

The key to improving health care for Medicare enrollees and reducing the burden Medicare imposes on taxpayers is to make that voucher explicit and as flexible as possible—that is, to subsidize Medicare enrollees with cash and trust them to spend it, just as Social Security does.

A Result, and a Font, of Government Failure

Congress created Medicare in 1965 to fix a problem that Congress itself created. By 1964, private health insurance that covered workers into retirement was widely available.[3] More than 70 insurance companies offered such coverage and "many Americans over sixty-five were covered by health insurance policies that were guaranteed renewable for life."[4] Yet only one-third to one-half of seniors had meaningful health insurance. Why?

For 45 years leading up to 1965, the federal tax code *penalized* workers if they purchased seamless health insurance plans that covered them into retirement.[5] In 1964, the federal government wrote, "Several factors contribute to th[e] lack of coverage among elderly people," in particular, "many of these persons who had insurance coverage before retirement were unable to retain the coverage after retirement . . . because the policy was available to employed persons only."[6] (See Chapter 10.)

Rather than fix the underlying problem that Congress itself created, Congress created Medicare, which made the underlying problem worse.

Low-Quality Medical Care

Much of the $1 trillion Medicare spends each year goes toward medical care that provides at least some value to patients. It would be difficult even for the federal government to spend that much money without producing any benefit. Yet Medicare spends vast sums on medical care that provides little or no benefit to patients. Medicare subsidies encourage the consumption of low-value care, while the rules Congress attaches to those subsidies reward low-quality care and discourage many quality improvements.

An enormous portion of what Medicare spends appears to produce no benefit at all. The *Dartmouth Atlas of Health Care* and other research estimate that one-third or more of Medicare spending provides no value whatsoever: it makes the patient no healthier or happier.[7] Those estimates relate to medical services that provide *zero* net value; they do not include spending on services that provide some benefit but where the benefits are so small that the patient would rather have spent the money on something else. Including those expenditures, even more than one-third of Medicare spending is wasteful.

One potential reason so much Medicare spending does not benefit patients is that Medicare has had a profound negative impact on health care quality. Medicare notoriously pays providers more for low-quality care and less for high-quality care.[8] In 2003, the Medicare Payment Advisory Commission warned Congress: "In the Medicare program, the payment system is largely neutral or negative towards quality. . . . At times providers are paid even more when quality is worse, such as when complications occur as the result of error."[9] A 2016 study, for example, found that Medicare paid low-quality hospitals an average of $2,698 more per patient than it paid high-quality hospitals.[10]

A landmark study by economists Amy Finkelstein and Robin McKnight found that, although Medicare undoubtedly purchases some life-saving medical care, it does not appear to have saved any lives in its first 10 years and that on balance it may produce no net societal benefits:

> Using several different empirical approaches, we find no evidence that the introduction of nearly universal health insurance for the elderly had an impact on overall elderly mortality in its first 10 years. . . . Our findings suggest that Medicare did not play a role in the substantial declines in elderly mortality that immediately followed the introduction of Medicare.[11]

In other words, from 1966 through 1975, Medicare appears to have spent $333 *billion* on medical care without saving a single life.[12] Data limitations prevented the authors from estimating any other potential health benefits from that spending. The authors nevertheless found the benefits of reducing out-of-pocket medical spending among seniors could justify no more than 40 percent of Medicare's cost. The study raises the very real prospect that Medicare *as a whole* has been net harmful to society.

Higher Taxes, Prices, Premiums, and Spending

Though Medicare heavily subsidizes medical care for its enrollees, it makes health care harder for nonenrollees to afford. Medicare has dramatically increased taxes, private-sector medical prices, and premiums for private health insurance.

To keep pace with explosive Medicare spending, Congress has increased taxes on workers an average of once every two years.[13] In part, this increase is to finance vast quantities of low- and zero-value medical care. Medicare also forces taxpayers to cover the excessive prices the program pays for low- and high-value care alike. Ambulatory surgical centers perform cataract surgeries for an average $1,000, for example, yet Medicare pays hospital outpatient departments an average $2,000 for the same services.[14] The federal government reports, "The Medicare program pays nearly twice as much as it would pay for the same or similar drugs in other countries."[15] From 2010 through 2017, the excessive prices Medicare paid hospitals for evaluation and management services in just eight states cost taxpayers at least $1.3 billion and enrollees in those states $334 million.[16]

Medicare even drives up prices in the private sector, sticking nonenrollees with higher prices for everything from drugs to physician services.[17] Economist Martin Feldstein found that "after introduction of Medicare and Medicaid, physicians' fees rose at 6.8 percent per year in 1967 and 1968 in comparison to a 3.2 percent annual rise in [prices]," while hospital prices increased by nearly 15 percent per year from 1966 to 1970.[18] Those higher prices increase private insurance premiums.

Medicare also increases the volume of services nonenrollees receive, which further increases private health insurance premiums. Finkelstein found evidence that Medicare increased *total* hospital spending by 37 percent within five years. Much of that increase—perhaps 16 percentage points, or nearly half of the effect—was because Medicare increased hospital spending among *non*enrollees. How? When the average level of insurance coverage rises, providers treat all patients more intensively. "For example," Finkelstein writes, "if Medicare induces a hospital to incur the fixed cost of adopting a new technology, the new technology, once adopted, may also be used on nonelderly individuals."[19] Medicare subsidies for elderly patients thus increased prices, health spending, and insurance premiums for nonelderly patients. Finkelstein further found that "the impact of Medicare on health spending rises over the second five years of its existence."[20]

Efforts to improve quality or reduce spending in Medicare generally have not been successful.[21]

Apply "Public Option" Principles to Medicare

Congress can reduce the burden Medicare imposes on taxpayers and reverse Medicare's negative impact on quality by applying traditionally Democratic "public option" principles to the program, such that traditional Medicare and private insurers compete on as level a playing field as possible.

One consequence of the mind-boggling complexity of medicine is that no single method of paying health care providers or organizing the delivery of medical care is capable of containing all costs or rewarding all dimensions of quality. Doing both requires open competition on a level playing field between different payment rules and modes of delivery. Public-option principles demand exactly that: a level playing field where consumers are the ultimate arbiters of quality and efficiency. Heavily favoring just one method of payment or delivery system, as Medicare does, predictably and persistently leads to excessive costs, rewards certain forms of low-quality care, and discourages improvement on those dimensions of quality.

Traditional Medicare is a government-run plan that already competes against private insurers. Economist Mark Pauly explains that Medicare "is essentially a risk-adjusted voucher program" that lets enrollees choose between a public option and private Medicare Advantage plans.[22]

That playing field, however, is anything but level. Congress bars certain plans and tilts the playing field toward excessive coverage and against high-quality coverage. It further violates public-option principles by offering larger subsidies to healthy enrollees if they choose Medicare Advantage while offering larger subsidies to sicker enrollees if they choose traditional Medicare.

Public-option principles demand eliminating all such distortions, including the benefits mandates and community-rating price controls Congress imposes on private health insurance plans that serve Medicare enrollees.

Most important, public-option principles require that each enrollee's subsidy neither rise nor fall depending on which health plan, or how much coverage, the enrollee chooses. Only one type of subsidy can do that: cash.

Public-option principles thus require that Medicare mirror Social Security, which gives enrollees cash and trusts them to spend it. In 2022, Medicare spent enough to give each enrollee an average cash subsidy of $12,100. Income- and risk-adjustment would give poorer and sicker enrollees thousands more than the average enrollee to ensure they could afford coverage.

Enrollees would spend that money better than government bureaucrats do. Evidence shows that cost-conscious patients force providers to reduce prices (see Figure 11.1) and that when seniors control their health decisions, even those with cognitive limitations make good choices.[23]

Figure 11.1
Price-conscious patients lower prices: Average price reductions within two years of patients becoming price-conscious

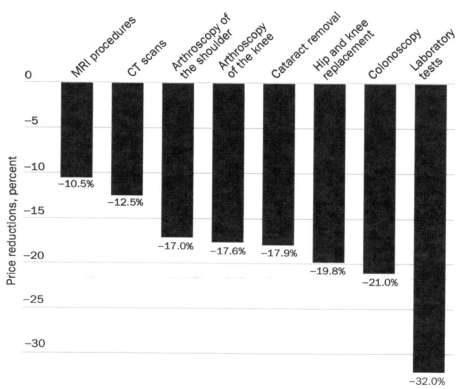

Source: James Robinson, Timothy Brown, and Christopher Whaley, "Reference Pricing Changes the 'Choice Archtecture' of Health Care for Consumers," *Health Affairs* 36, no. 3 (March 2017): 524–30.

The size of individual enrollees' Medicare checks should vary with health status and income. When an individual enrolls, Medicare should use competitive bidding and its current risk-adjustment program to adjust the amount of the enrollee's check according to that individual enrollee's health status. It should use Social Security Administration data to adjust the amount of the enrollee's check according to the enrollee's lifetime income. Low-income and sicker enrollees would get Medicare checks large enough to enable them to afford a standard package of insurance benefits; healthier and higher-income enrollees would get smaller checks.

Congress should restrain overall Medicare spending by limiting per-enrollee spending to gross domestic product growth. Health care prices would likely fall so dramatically that Congress could reduce Medicare spending growth even more without harming access or enrollee health.

Critics worry that if risk adjustment is imperfect, some enrollees would have insufficient funds to purchase health plans. But Medicare's imperfect risk-adjustment formulas are already harming sick enrollees by punishing Medicare Advantage plans that provide high-quality coverage to those enrollees. Subsidizing enrollees with cash would benefit sick enrollees by reducing prices and creating incentives for insurers to find innovative ways to cover the sick, rather than to avoid them.

Prefund Retiree Health Care

After converting Medicare to a Social Security–like cash-transfer program, Congress should replace Medicare's inequitable system of intergenerational transfers with a system in which workers invest their Medicare taxes in personal accounts for their health needs in retirement.

Congress should allow workers to put their full Medicare payroll tax payment (generally 2.9 percent of earnings) in a personal savings account. Workers could invest those funds in a number of vehicles and augment those funds in retirement with other savings. For most workers, those savings could replace the subsidies they receive through Medicare. Over time, Congress could make contributions to these personal accounts voluntary.

As with some Social Security reform proposals, diverting workers' payroll tax payments into personal accounts would reduce federal revenues, making it more difficult to finance current Medicare subsidies. Public-option principles would go a long way toward solving this problem by reducing health care prices and encouraging enrollees to eliminate wasteful medical consumption, each of which would enable Congress to reduce overall Medicare outlays significantly. To the extent that these efficiency gains do not cover all transition costs, Congress should make up the gap by cutting other government spending—not by raising taxes.

12. MEDICAID AND THE CHILDREN'S HEALTH INSURANCE PROGRAM

States should

- reduce spending on Medicaid and the Children's Health Insurance Program (CHIP, previously the State Children's Health Insurance Program or SCHIP) whenever possible;
- refuse to implement the Medicaid expansion provisions of the Patient Protection and Affordable Care Act (ACA or Obamacare);
- conduct randomized, controlled experiments of the effects of Medicaid and CHIP on existing populations;
- reduce unmet medical need by deregulating medical care and health insurance; and
- demand that the federal government grant states flexibility with existing Medicaid and CHIP funds—not additional funds—to provide medical and long-term care to the needy.

Congress should

- eliminate or reform the tax exclusion for employer-sponsored health insurance;
- turn Medicare into a Social Security–like cash-transfer program;
- repeal Obamacare;
- deregulate health care and health insurance;
- permit states to conduct randomized, controlled experiments on the effects of Medicaid and CHIP coverage on existing populations;
- eliminate federal entitlements to Medicaid and CHIP benefits;
- freeze each state's Medicaid and CHIP funding at current-year levels;
- give states full flexibility to use Medicaid and CHIP funds to achieve a few broad goals; and
- begin phasing out Medicaid and CHIP federal funding.

The greatest economic safety net humans have devised is the market. A market system uses innovation to fill the cracks in the health care sector so that fewer vulnerable patients fall through with every passing day. It brings health care of ever-increasing quality within reach of an ever-increasing number of people. It drives prices for medical care and health insurance downward. It harnesses the self-interest of clinicians, administrators, insurers, and other patients to improve the quality of medical care and health insurance. It minimizes the problem of preexisting conditions.

When government tries to fill in the cracks in the health sector, it creates new ones and causes existing cracks to widen. After decades of government making medical care and health insurance more expensive with interventions like Medicare, the tax exclusion for employer-sponsored health insurance, and licensing of clinicians and health insurance, far fewer low- and middle-income households can access health care than could in a market system.

Unfortunately, the government's response has been to intervene even further. As with Medicare, Congress created Medicaid and CHIP to solve problems that Congress itself either exacerbated or caused. Those programs have in turn further increased tax burdens and the cost of health care.

The most important thing policymakers can do to improve access to care for the poor is not to subsidize care, but to liberalize the health care sector. Liberalizing the U.S. health care sector would do more to reduce unmet medical need than expanding or maintaining existing safety-net programs. It would make the problem of unmet need smaller and leave the rest of society wealthier and better able to help the shrinking number of patients who still could not help themselves.

The most important thing that policymakers can do to help the poor obtain health insurance and medical care is to adopt policies that spur cost-saving innovations and lower prices. Falling prices are progressive: they benefit the poor more than the rich. Moreover, they do not involve a "Samaritan's dilemma." Whereas welfare can trap the poor in poverty, falling prices help them climb out. The reforms that would put the most downward pressure on health care prices are turning Medicare into a Social Security–like cash-transfer program (see Chapter 11), reforming the tax treatment of health care (see Chapter 10), and deregulating medicine (see Chapters 5–8) and health insurance (see Chapter 9).

In addition, federal and state governments operate three main programs to provide medical care to low-income Americans: Medicaid, CHIP, and premium subsidies available through the health insurance "Exchanges" of Obamacare. Congress should repeal or fundamentally reform each of these programs.

Medicaid

Medicaid spends $834 billion annually, ostensibly to provide health care to the poor.[1] The federal government jointly administers Medicaid with state and territorial governments.

States that wish to participate in Medicaid must pay a portion of the cost of a federally defined set of health benefits to a federally defined population of eligible individuals. All states participate in the traditional Medicaid program, which primarily serves four low-income groups: mothers and their children, the disabled, the elderly, and those needing long-term care. Specific eligibility criteria vary by state, as does the exact rate at which the federal government matches state spending on Medicaid.

Overall, the federal government finances 65 percent of total Medicaid outlays, while states finance 35 percent.[2] In return for participating in Medicaid and financing a portion of program spending, each state receives matching federal funds to administer its program. When states spend money on mandatory populations—or make Medicaid benefits more comprehensive, or extend eligibility to more people than the federal government requires—the federal government matches what states spend, seemingly without limit.

Obamacare gives states the option to expand their Medicaid programs to all adults with incomes below 138 percent of the federal poverty level. (The federal poverty level, and thus Medicaid-expansion eligibility thresholds rise with the number of household members and with time. As of 2022, the Medicaid-expansion eligibility threshold was $18,754 for single adults.) The principal beneficiaries of Obamacare's Medicaid expansion are able-bodied adults. Starting in 2014, the federal government paid 100 percent of the cost of a state's expansion population, gradually declining to 90 percent in 2020. Despite multiple attempts to sweeten the deal with additional federal matching funds, 10 states still refused to implement Obamacare's Medicaid expansion in 2022.

For beneficiaries, Medicaid is an entitlement. So long as they meet the eligibility criteria, they have a legally enforceable claim to benefits. People tend to cycle on and off Medicaid for various reasons. The federal government estimates that 79 million people will enroll in Medicaid during 2023.[3]

Perverse Incentives

Financing Medicaid by having the federal government match state spending encourages fraud, creates perverse incentives for state officials, and encourages states to enroll people who don't need assistance. Because federal and state governments share the burden of Medicaid spending, neither side cares about waste, fraud, or induced dependence as much as they should—or would—care if either were to bear 100 percent of the cost.

The more a state spends on its Medicaid program, the more it receives in federal matching funds. When a state spends $1, it receives between $1 and $9. States can thus receive a double, triple, or even ninefold return when they devote state funds to Medicaid rather than other priorities like education or roads.

Medicaid's matching-grant system encourages astounding amounts of fraud. The Government Accountability Office consistently designates Medicaid as a "high-risk" program, estimating that "Medicaid improper payments represented 21.4 percent of federal program spending—more than $85 billion—in fiscal year 2020."[4]

The system creates perverse incentives for state officials to divert funds away from higher-value uses. Spending $1 on police buys $1 of police protection. Spending $1 on Medicaid, however, buys $2 to $10 of medical or long-term care. Medicaid rewards states for spending the marginal dollar on medical and long-term care even when spending it on police, education, or transportation would provide greater benefit.

It also encourages states to cut other priorities to protect Medicaid spending. Unlike the federal government, nearly all state legislatures face constitutional or statutory requirements to balance their operating budgets each year. States that try to do so by reducing state spending must cut "old" Medicaid outlays by $2 million to $5 million or cut Medicaid expansion outlays by $10 million to achieve just $1 million of budgetary savings. Medicaid encourages states to cut spending on police, education, and transportation, where $1 million in budgetary savings inflicts only $1 million of political pain, rather than on Medicaid, where $1 million in budgetary savings requires inflicting $2 million to $10 million of political pain.

Obamacare's Medicaid expansion created additional perverse incentives to prioritize able-bodied adults over more vulnerable enrollees. If states cut spending on mothers and children, the disabled, the elderly, and long-term care recipients, then achieving $1 million in budgetary savings requires inflicting $2 million to $5 million of political pain. Achieving the same savings by cutting spending on able-bodied adults requires inflicting $10 million of political pain.

Medicaid both pulls and pushes enrollees into dependence. Medicaid pushes people into dependence on government for their health care by making private health care less affordable. Economists Mark Duggan of Stanford and Fiona Scott Morton of Yale found, for example, that Medicaid's system of setting drug prices increases prices for private payers by 15 percent.[5] The more federal and state governments expand Medicaid, the more expensive private medical care and health insurance become. Medicaid pulls enrollees into dependence on government by offering a valuable subsidy that disappears as income rises. Enrollees often see little or no economic benefit to working harder and increasing their incomes, which creates a powerful disincentive to becoming financially independent.

The Children's Health Insurance Program

Congress created CHIP in 1997 to expand health insurance coverage among children in families that earn too much to be eligible for Medicaid. The federal government funds each state's program much as it funds traditional Medicaid but with two main differences. First, states receive a larger federal match under CHIP than under traditional Medicaid. In 2022, the federal government will have financed at least 69 percent of the cost of each state's program. For every dollar that states invest in CHIP, they receive on average about $3 from the federal government—that is, from taxpayers in other states.

Second, the federal government ostensibly limits the amount it will contribute to each state's program, but the cap is not as binding as it appears. States often burn through their federal CHIP funds before the end of the fiscal year and then demand additional funds. In effect, states *create* emergencies and then demand emergency funding, in effect daring Congress to deny their demands, which would strip coverage from sick children. Congress has repeatedly bailed out states that employ that gambit, which effectively rewards states for committing to spend more federal dollars than federal law allows.

As a result of these perverse incentives, states have expanded CHIP eligibility dramatically. Eighteen states and the District of Columbia offer CHIP to families of four with annual incomes of $83,000 or more.[6] In New York, CHIP is available to families of four earning $112,000 annually. Because CHIP targets families higher up the income scale than Medicaid does, and because higher-income families are more likely to have health insurance to begin with, CHIP leads to an even greater crowding out of private insurance than that caused by Medicaid.

Are Medicaid and CHIP Even Helping?

Remarkably, there is little reliable evidence that these programs have a net positive effect on health and no evidence that they are the best way to improve the health of targeted populations.

In 2008, the Oregon Health Insurance Experiment examined the effects of Medicaid by taking advantage of a policy that randomly assigned applicants to receive Medicaid or nothing and then compared outcomes for the two groups. As it happens, the study examined a population that would receive coverage under Obamacare's Medicaid expansion. Random assignment made this experiment the most reliable study ever conducted on the effects of health insurance. The authors found that Medicaid coverage "did increase use of health care services, raise rates of diabetes detection and management, lower rates of depression, and reduce financial strain." But even though researchers chose measures of physical health that were amenable to treatment over a two-year period, Medicaid enrollment "generated no significant improvements in measured physical health outcomes in the first 2 years."[7] The lack of any improvement in physical health outcomes among Medicaid enrollees should throw a stop sign in front of Medicaid generally and Obamacare's Medicaid expansion in particular.

Similarly, there is no evidence that Medicaid is cost-effective. The Oregon Health Insurance Experiment did find small improvements in self-reported mental health. But that study did not attempt to quantify whether Medicaid is a cost-effective way of achieving those gains—that is, whether state and federal governments could have purchased better health by spending those funds differently or enacting different reforms. Federal and state governments should not continue to take trillions of dollars from taxpayers to support those programs when they don't even know what they are getting in return.

Whether or not Medicaid, CHIP, or Obamacare's premium subsidies turn out to improve health for some populations, or to be a cost-effective way of doing so, these programs become increasingly less cost-effective the higher up the income scale they reach. Higher-income households have higher baseline access to health insurance and medical care. As these programs move up the income scale, they offer taxpayer-financed coverage to increasing numbers of people who already have private insurance. One study estimated Obamacare's Medicaid expansion would lead to "high rates of crowd-out for Medicaid expansions aimed at working adults (82 percent), suggesting that the Medicaid expansion provisions . . . will shift workers and their families from private to public insurance without reducing the number of uninsured very much."[8] That estimate suggests that Obamacare's Medicaid expansion could be covering fewer than 2 previously uninsured Americans for the price of 10.

Determine Whether Medicaid Actually Helps

Rather than expand Medicaid, federal and state policymakers should conduct further experiments to determine what benefits Medicaid and CHIP actually produce and whether other uses of those funds would produce greater gains in health and financial security. Policymakers should model those studies on the Oregon Health Insurance Experiment. States should conduct those studies with existing populations rather than new enrollees, so as not to impose additional burdens on taxpayers.

The federal government should grant waivers to states that conduct such studies. Where federal law does not provide authority for the Secretary of Health and Human Services to approve such waivers, Congress should grant it or enact legislation directly approving such studies.

Block Obamacare's Medicaid Expansion

States that have implemented Obamacare's Medicaid expansion are buckling under the expense. In those states, enrollment and per-enrollee spending have exceeded projections.[9]

The 10 states that have still refused to implement Obamacare's Medicaid expansion in 2022 should continue to refuse to do so. States that have implemented it should withdraw from the program—or at least conduct randomized experiments to determine what the program is delivering.

Repeal Obamacare

Congress should repeal Obamacare's Medicaid expansion along with the rest of that law. Repealing the Medicaid expansion alone would reduce federal spending and deficits by $1.5 trillion from 2024 through 2033 and eliminate the low-wage trap that program creates. Repealing the remainder of Obamacare would eliminate the low-wage traps its Exchange subsidies create and reduce federal spending and deficits by a further $1 trillion, while also reducing the cost of private health insurance for the vast majority of enrollees in those programs.[10]

If the Medicaid expansion were popular, states would be willing to pay for it themselves. Not only did zero states take that step, but 10 states have rejected it, even with Congress pledging to pick up 90 percent of the tab. States that have rejected the Medicaid expansion have restrained federal spending, federal deficits, and the future tax burden of taxpayers in *all* states, saving taxpayers hundreds of billions of dollars. It is unfair to force taxpayers in states that have rejected the Medicaid expansion to pay for the expansion in other states.

Medicaid and CHIP

Repealing Obamacare is not enough, however. It makes little sense for taxpayers to send money to Washington only for Congress to send those funds back to their state capitols with strings and perverse incentives. Congress should devolve control over Medicaid and CHIP to the states.

In 1996, Congress eliminated the federal entitlement to a welfare check, placed a five-year limit on cash assistance, and froze federal spending on such assistance. It then distributed those funds to the states in the form of block grants with fewer federal restrictions. The results were unquestionably positive. Welfare rolls fell by half, and poverty reached the lowest point in a generation.

The federal government should emulate that success by eliminating all federal entitlements to Medicaid and CHIP benefits, freezing federal Medicaid and CHIP spending at current levels, and distributing those funds to the states as unrestricted block grants. Block grants like those Congress used to reform cash assistance would eliminate the perverse incentives that induce dependence and that encourage states to favor Medicaid and CHIP spending over other priorities, to tolerate widespread fraud, and to defraud federal taxpayers. Congressional Budget Office projections indicate that simply freezing remaining federal Medicaid and CHIP spending at 2024 levels would produce $3.1 trillion in savings and deficit reduction by 2033.

With full flexibility and full responsibility for the marginal Medicaid dollar, states could then decide whether and how to navigate the Samaritan's dilemma. States that want to focus only on their neediest residents could do so and put the savings toward other priorities or tax reduction. States that want to spend more on their Medicaid programs would be free to raise taxes to do so, and vice versa. States would learn from the successes and failures of each other's experiments. Since states would bear the full marginal cost of their reformed Medicaid programs or successor programs, they would be more likely to conduct randomized, controlled experiments to determine the most cost-effective uses of those funds.

Over time, the federal government should give the states full responsibility for Medicaid by eliminating federal Medicaid spending while concomitantly cutting federal taxes. States can hasten these reforms by pressuring the federal government for maximum flexibility in administering their Medicaid programs.

13. VETERANS HEALTH CARE

Congress should

- direct federal actuaries to publish annual present-value estimates of the long-term cost of all veterans-benefits obligations, plus the market value of all Veterans Health Administration (VHA) assets;
- increase military pay to allow all active-duty military personnel to purchase, at actuarially fair rates, a standard package of private life, disability, and health insurance benefits comparable to those the Department of Veterans Affairs provides;
- privatize VHA facilities, financial capital, and physical capital by transferring ownership to veterans; and
- deliver benefits to current VHA-eligible veterans via risk-adjusted payments.

The Department of Veterans Affairs (VA) is never more than a few months away from scandal for the often poor service it provides veterans. Yet the reality of how the VA disserves veterans and even active-duty military personnel is far worse than the headlines suggest.

Overview

Veterans benefits are a form of compensation the U.S. government provides to employees of the U.S. armed forces. Benefits include life, disability, and health insurance, as well as assistance with housing, education, training, and rehabilitation. The VA will spend roughly $305 billion in 2023 to provide benefits to veterans, survivors, and dependents who meet various criteria.[1]

The wars in Afghanistan and Iraq have caused a surge in spending on veterans benefits. "Federal expenditures to care for veterans doubled from 2.4 percent of the U.S. budget in FY 2001 to 4.9 percent in FY 2020, even as the total number of living veterans from all U.S. wars declined from 25.3 million to 18.5 million."[2]

The VA provides health care directly to beneficiaries through the Veterans Health Administration, an integrated health care delivery system. The VHA "operates the largest integrated health care . . . system in the Nation, with more than 1,700 hospitals, clinics, and other health care facilities."[3] In 2023, the VHA will employ 370,000 people and spend roughly $128 billion to provide medical care to 7.4 million patients.[4] Ironically, the U.S. government operates the nation's largest integrated delivery system at the same time it suppresses private integrated health systems (see Chapters 5–7 and 9–11).

Congress determines overall funding for veterans benefits and the allocation of VHA resources.

Quality

The VHA appears to outperform private health care providers on some quality measures. Studies generally find that the VHA does better on process measures of quality, such as providing evidence-based care, but no better on outcomes, such as risk-adjusted mortality.[5] Yet such studies typically compare two types of government-run systems, rather than comparing a government-run system against a market system.[6] The tax code, Medicare, Medicaid, and other government interventions give the government a comparable degree of control over "private" hospitals. Such studies say little about whether a market system would perform better or worse than a government-run system.

The quality of all VA benefits suffers because government administration of those benefits exposes veterans to political risk: veterans can lose benefits at the whim of politicians and bureaucrats. Health coverage cannot be high quality if it is not secure. If Congress adopts various Congressional Budget Office proposals to reduce VA spending, millions of veterans would see their VHA benefits disappear.[7] If and when Congress ever gets serious about reducing federal deficits, it could terminate benefits for even more veterans.

An Unresponsive Bureaucracy

The most notorious example of poor quality at the VHA is long waits for care. Wait times are longer in some areas and tend to persist because the VHA does not have a price mechanism to move resources from low- to high-value uses. Congress and the VA use a combination of politics and bureaucratic rationing to decide when and where to open and close VHA facilities, or how many clinicians to hire in each region of the country. The result is inevitable and persistent mismatches between demand and supply—shortages in some areas and gluts in others.

In 2014, whistleblowers and watchdogs discovered that 60 percent of VHA facilities were falsifying official records to make wait times appear shorter.[8] Veterans at one facility in Phoenix were waiting 115 days for appointments.[9] Congress responded with $5 billion to hire additional clinicians and expand VHA capacity, and $10 billion to pay for veterans to see private-sector doctors at taxpayers' expense. The additional bureaucracy associated with this option left many veterans waiting even longer than before.[10]

Despite a media firestorm, congressional oversight hearings, numerous VA officials losing their jobs, and federal legislation, in 2021 more than 810,000 veterans waited more than a month for appointments, while nearly 197,000 waited more than six months.[11] The problem of shortages and slow service extends beyond health benefits. In 2021, more than 215,000 veterans waited more than four months for disability and pension benefits determinations.[12] In addition, the VHA does not yet track appointments and wait times accurately. In 2019, the Government Accountability Office (GAO) reported that inaccuracies in the VHA's appointment scheduling processes hid the fact that "veterans could potentially wait up to 70 calendar days to see a [non-VHA] provider."[13]

The flip side of shortages is gluts. Political and bureaucratic constraints make it difficult for the VHA to shut down, sell, or repurpose facilities. The VHA has increasingly turned to leasing properties, a process that makes it easier to open, close, and repurpose facilities. Yet the VHA's secrecy makes it difficult to know whether this process is more or less efficient. According to the GAO, the "VA does not . . . assess and provide information to decision makers on how it has benefited from this flexibility. Without transparency on these benefits, VA and congressional decision makers may lack information to understand the need for these leases."[14]

Costs

Idle capital is just one of the costs of the VHA. Supporters claim that, for all its faults, the VHA provides care of comparable quality at a lower cost than Medicare or private insurance. The VHA's secrecy makes it difficult to make these comparisons. The Congressional Budget Office has testified to Congress:

> With few exceptions, VHA does not make either existing administrative data or clinical records (even with personal identifying information removed) available to researchers in other government agencies, universities, or elsewhere. . . . [I]t would be useful to know the average salaries, performance pay, and other elements of compensation that VHA provides for its physicians in various specialties and for its other clinicians; the number of patients its clinicians treat per unit of time (for example, in a typical week) and the length and

intensity of those encounters; and the average prices it pays for pharmaceutical products—but VHA does not report that information publicly.[15]

Even so, it would not be surprising if a health care system subject to bureaucratic rationing and tolerant of long waits for care had lower per unit costs, given the excessive prices government intervention allows to persist in the private sector (see Chapters 5–10) and Medicare (see Chapter 11).

The VA Encourages Unnecessary Wars

The greatest harms the VA inflicts on veterans stem not from the services it provides, but from how it helps Congress and the president start, enter, and perpetuate wars.

Veterans benefits are some of the most expensive financial costs of war. The VA reports that the present value of just the compensation and burial benefits that Congress has promised to current veterans reached $6.1 trillion as of 2022, which amounts to 24 percent of U.S. gross domestic product, more than the federal government collected in revenue, and nearly as much as total federal outlays ($6.3 trillion) for that year.[16] That $6.1 trillion unfunded-liability figure does not include the additional accrued liabilities of providing health care, long-term care, or life insurance benefits to veterans.

The majority of spending on veterans benefits occurs decades after Congress incurs those obligations. Disability payments, for example, typically do not peak until 30 to 40 years after the end of a military conflict.[17] "Since compensation benefits begin for a Veteran and continue through their survivors," the VA "issued American Civil War-era benefits payments as recently as 2020 when the last beneficiary passed away, 155 years after the end of the war. The beneficiary was the daughter of a soldier who fought first for the Confederacy and later for the Union during his service in the Civil War."[18] As of 2021, there were still 100 survivors receiving VA benefits in connection with World War I and prior wars, as well as 1.7 million veterans and survivors receiving benefits in connection with Vietnam-era service (1961–1975).[19]

Since the federal government does not fund veterans benefits until they come due, Congress and the president can commit U.S. armed forces to battle without having to pay or even acknowledge those costs. The VA enables elected officials who send U.S. troops to war to pretend that one of the largest financial costs of that decision does not exist.

If Congress funded those obligations as it accrued them, it would have to raise revenue every year to fund future veterans benefits. In years when it was sending troops into battle, Congress would have to raise even more revenue because future veterans benefits claims would be higher. Having to budget for the cost of those additional veterans benefits and then weigh those costs against other priorities would make Congress less likely to start, enter, or perpetuate wars. When the decision to authorize military force is a close call, having to finance those costs up front could prevent war.

Instead, the VA system allows Congress to ignore these costs. It thus eliminates a constraint that could prevent unnecessary wars. The very agency that exists to care for sick and disabled veterans and their survivors perversely makes it more likely that veterans will end up sick, disabled, or dead.

Report the Cost of Accrued Veterans Benefits

Requiring transparency about the cost of future veterans benefits would be an important step toward improving veterans benefits. Congress should immediately direct federal actuaries, at the GAO, the VA, or other agencies, to project and report regularly on the present-value cost of all veterans benefits obligations, just as the Social Security and Medicare trustees report on those programs' accrued obligations. Simply having better information would improve debates over veterans benefits, the U.S. military, and foreign policy.

Prefund Veterans Benefits

Congress must do more than make the current VA system transparent. Protecting veterans, active-duty personnel, and civilians requires a complete overhaul of veterans benefits. One reform would deliver better, more reliable benefits for veterans and force Congress and the president to make more careful decisions affecting the lives of active-duty personnel.

Congress should fund veterans benefits in advance by immediately increasing salaries for all active-duty personnel. All service members would receive a pay raise sufficient to allow them to purchase, from private insurers at actuarially fair rates, a statutorily defined package of life, disability, and health care benefits comparable with what the VA offers. Benefits would cover losses related to an enlistment or commission, beginning when service members leave active duty. Military personnel would be free to purchase more or less coverage than the standard benefits package. Upon leaving active duty, veterans could receive benefits from the insurance carriers and health care providers of their choice, rather than have no choice but a single government-run health care system.

Congress should use competitive bidding by insurers to determine the salary increases for active-duty personnel. Bids by insurers would allow Congress to peg pay raises for each job type to the actual premiums that competing insurers charge to cover personnel in each position. (Congress could peg salary increases to the second-lowest, median, or average premium bid.) Since insurers would be free to set actuarially fair premiums, premiums and the corresponding pay raises would be higher for paratroopers than desk jockeys, which would enable all personnel to afford the same package of benefits. The differences in premiums across job types would allow military personnel to compare the relative risks of different military jobs and careers.

This veteran-centered system would provide future veterans with better benefits. Rather than benefits that can disappear at the whim of politicians and bureaucrats, veterans would have a legally enforceable contract. If veterans lose their benefits under the current system, the government works against them. If they were to lose them under a veteran-centered system, the government would work with them to restore those benefits.

If things ever got that far. Private insurers and health care providers would be more responsive to veterans' needs under such a system—if they were not, veterans could fire them. Insurers who developed a reputation for mistreating veterans comparable to that of the VA would have a difficult time enrolling new active-duty personnel. If Congress privatized the VHA system by transferring ownership to veterans themselves (see next section), then veterans would have the option of using an integrated health system run by veterans, for veterans.

Most important, prefunding veterans benefits in this manner would make Congress and the president more cautious about using military force. Military action would cause insurers to increase premiums for life, disability, and health benefits to cover the increased risk. Those higher premiums would trigger mandatory salary increases for military personnel. Not only would this be a more honest and transparent way of providing veterans benefits, but also Congress and the president would be more cautious about engaging in military action because they would have to give up more to get it. Revealing the costs of war to policymakers can *only* lead to better decisions about when to begin and end wars.

Putting those funds directly in the hands of military personnel is an indispensable component of a prefunded system. Creating yet another government trust fund would merely allow Congress to continue to hide this cost of war.

A prefunded system of veterans benefits could also aid recruiting. It would give military personnel more information about various jobs and more peace of mind about their veterans benefits. Competition among insurers and providers for cost-conscious active-duty personnel and veterans would help drive private health care prices downward.

Privatize VHA Facilities

To reward current veterans and to enable even greater competition in the provision of their medical benefits, Congress should privatize VHA facilities by transferring ownership of the VHA to veterans themselves. Privatization would be a large wealth transfer to veterans. The VA estimated the value of its real assets (physical capital and investments) at $36 billion in 2021.[20]

Congress should incorporate the VHA and give ownership shares to VHA-eligible veterans on the basis of income, length of service, reliance on VA benefits, or similar criteria. The exact manner in which Congress transfers ownership of the VHA system to veterans is less important than its doing so as soon as possible.

Veteran-shareholders would then select a management team, perhaps from current VHA personnel, veterans groups, private health systems, and insurers or other financial institutions with a record of serving military personnel. A privatized VHA could continue to serve only veterans or opt to serve nonveteran patients, and thereby enrich its veteran-shareholders. The VHA could pursue different strategies in different parts of the country.

Privatization of the VHA could improve health care for veterans and non-veterans alike. Because the VHA is the largest integrated health system in the nation, privatizing it would force incumbent health care providers to compete with a financing and delivery system that does not exist in most markets.

Choice for Current VHA Enrollees

To maintain benefits for current veterans after privatization, Congress should provide risk-adjusted payments that enable VHA-eligible veterans to purchase a comparable level of health coverage from private providers. This approach could be similar to the salary increases for active-duty personnel or the Medicare reforms in Chapter 11. With risk adjustment, current veterans could afford to purchase health coverage at actuarially fair premiums.

Liberalizing and privatizing veterans benefits will result in better, more affordable, and more secure health care for veterans. Most important, it would protect active-duty personnel from harm by forcing Congress and the president to make more careful decisions about whether and when to engage in military conflicts.

14. CONCLUSION

In the 1950s—before there was Obamacare or the Children's Health Insurance Program, or even Medicare and Medicaid—the economist Milton Friedman made a prediction. If government simply stopped interfering in the market for medical care, markets would do a better job of meeting people's health care needs than the government was doing then, or could ever do.

Friedman, who would go on to win the Nobel Prize in economics, predicted with remarkable prescience that entrepreneurs would develop the very sort of quality-improving and cost-reducing innovations that they *have* developed, that government has suppressed and continues to suppress, and that centralized government planners are still struggling to replicate themselves.

Health policy scholars may recognize the innovations Friedman predicted:

> Suppose that anyone had been free to practice medicine without restriction except for legal and financial responsibility for any harm done to others through fraud and negligence. I conjecture that the whole development of medicine would have been different. The present market for medical care, hampered as it has been, gives some hints of what the difference would have been. Group practice in conjunction with hospitals would have grown enormously. Instead of individual practice plus large institutional hospitals conducted by governments or eleemosynary institutions, there might have developed medical partnerships or corporations—medical teams. These would have provided central diagnostic and treatment facilities, including hospital facilities. Some presumably would have been prepaid, combining in one package present hospital insurance, health insurance, and group medical practice. Others would have charged separate fees for separate services. And of course, most might have used both methods of payment.

> These medical teams—department stores of medicine, if you will—would be intermediaries between the patients and the physician. Being long-lived and immobile, they would have a great interest in establishing a reputation for reliability and quality. For the same reason, consumers would get to know their reputation. They would have the specialized skill to judge the quality of physicians; indeed, they would be the agent of the consumer in doing so, as

the department store is now for many a product. In addition, they could organize medical care efficiently, combining medical men of different degrees of skill and training, using technicians with limited training for tasks for which they were suited, and reserving highly skilled and competent specialists for the tasks they alone could perform.[1]

Friedman identified regulation as an obstacle to coordinated care, right-skilling, and other innovations that health policy makers are unsuccesfully attempting to deliver to patients via government direction.[2]

Since the 1950s, state and federal lawmakers have dramatically increased government's footprint in health care far beyond what it was when Friedman wrote those words. As a result, rather than bring these innovations to patients, government has made them more elusive than ever.

Day after day, U.S. patients suffer the consequences of a century of mounting government failures. American health care is worse, more dangerous, more expensive, and less secure than what a market system would deliver. Helping as many of the most vulnerable patients as possible requires repealing *all* the barriers government places in the way of better, more affordable, more secure health care. It requires replacing America's dysfunctional government-run health system with a market system. Policymakers who seek better health care for the most vulnerable must consider the reforms this book offers.

NOTES

Chapter 1

[1] Glen Whitman and Raymond Raad, "Bending the Productivity Curve: Why America Leads the World in Medical Innovation," Cato Institute Policy Analysis no. 654, November 18, 2009.

Chapter 2

[1] "Health Spending (Indicator): Total/Government/Compulsory, Voluntary, US dollars/capita, 2022 or latest available," Organisation for Economic Co-operation and Development (OECD); and "Health Spending (Indicator): Total, US dollars/capita, 1970–2021," OECD.

[2] "Health Spending (Indicator): Total/Government/Compulsory"; and "Health Spending (Indicator): Total, % of GDP, 2022 or latest available," OECD.

[3] John A. Poisal et al., "National Health Expenditure Projections 2021–30: Growth to Moderate as COVID-19 Impacts Wane," *Health Affairs* 41, no. 4 (March 28, 2022); "Gross Domestic Product (Indicator): Total, US Dollars/Capita, 2021 or Latest Available," OECD; and "Gross Domestic Product (Indicator): Total, Million US dollars, 2021 or latest available," OECD.

[4] "Gross Domestic Product (Indicator): Total, US Dollars/Capita"; and "Gross Domestic Product (Indicator): Total, Million US Dollars."

[5] Plus, obviously, the United States (2021 GDP: $23 trillion). "Gross Domestic Product (Indicator): Total, US Dollars/Capita"; and "Gross Domestic Product (Indicator): Total, Million US Dollars."

[6] Glen Whitman and Raymond Raad, "Bending the Productivity Curve: Why America Leads the World in Medical Innovation," Cato Institute Policy Analysis no. 654, November 18, 2009.

[7] "Hepatitis C," World Health Organization, June 24, 2022.

[8] Brian R. Edlin et al., "Toward a More Accurate Estimate of the Prevalence of Hepatitis C in the United States," *Hepatology* 62, no. 5 (October 20, 2015): 1353-63, https://doi.org/10.1002/hep.27978.

[9] Robert Preidt, "Study: New Hepatitis Meds Are Saving Lives," HealthDay News, February 12, 2019.

[10] "Does Sovaldi Cure Hepatitis C?," Drugs.com, last updated April 14, 2023.

[11] "Exposure to direct-acting antivirals was associated with a decrease in all-cause mortality (adjusted HR 0.48, 95% CI 0.33–0.70) and hepatocellular carcinoma (0.66, 0.46–0.93)." Fabrice Carrat et al., "Clinical Outcomes in Patients with Chronic Hepatitis C after Direct-Acting Antiviral Treatment: A Prospective Cohort Study," *The Lancet* 393, no. 10179 (April 6, 2019): 1453–64, https://doi.org/10.1016/S0140-6736(18)32111-1.

[12] Jerome L. Schwartz, "Early History of Prepaid Medical Care Plans," *Bulletin of the History of Medicine* 39, no. 5 (September–October 1965).

[13] Edward H. Wagner, Nirmala Sandhu, and Katherine M. Newton, "Effect of Improved Glycemic Control on Health Care Costs and Utilization," *JAMA* 285, no. 2 (January 10, 2001): 182–89.

[14] David J. Graham et al., "Risk of Acute Myocardial Infraction and Sudden Cardiac Death in Patients Treated with Cyclo-oxygenase 2 Selective and Non-selective Non-steroidal Anti-Inflammatory Drugs: Nested Case-Control Study," *The Lancet* 365, no. 9458 (February 5, 2005): 475–481, https://doi.org/10.1016/S0140-6736(05)17864-7.

[15] Clayton M. Christensen, Jerome Grossman, and Jason Hwang, *The Innovator's Prescription: A Disruptive Solution for Health Care* (New York: McGraw-Hill, 2009).

[16] Marcia Frellick, "15 Docs Fired from Illinois Health System to Be Replaced with NPs," *Medscape Medical News*, November 27, 2019.

[17] Grant R. Martsolf et al., "Employment of Advanced Practice Clinicians in Physician Practices," *JAMA Internal Medicine* 178, no. 7 (2018): 988–90.

[18] Tara Bannow, "Oregon Nurse Practitioners Can Now Perform Vasectomies," *The Bulletin*, August 1, 2017.

[19] Ashley N. Carranza, Pamela J. Munoz, and Angela J. Nash, "Comparing Quality of Care in Medical Specialties Between Nurse Practitioners and Physicians," *Journal of the American Association of Nurse Practitioners* 33, no. 3 (May 6, 2020):184–93, https://doi.org/10.1097/jxx.0000000000000394; R. M. A. van Erp et al., "Physician Assistants and Nurse Practitioners in Primary Care Plus: A Systematic Review," *International Journal of Integrated Care* 21, no. 1, (February 12, 2021): 6, https://doi.org/10.5334/ijic.5485; and Ellen T. Kurtzman and Burt S. Barnow, "A Comparison of Nurse Practitioners, Physician Assistants, and Primary Care Physicians' Patterns of Practice and Quality of Care in Health Centers," *Medical Care* 55, no. 6 (June 2017): 615–22, https://doi.org/10.1097/mlr.0000000000000689.

[20] Chuan-Fen Liu et al., "Outcomes of Primary Care Delivery by Nurse Practitioners: Utilization, Cost, and Quality of Care," *Health Services Research* 55, no. 2 (April 2020): 178–89, https://doi.org/10.1111/1475-6773.13246.

[21] MedPAC, "Chapter 5: Ambulatory Surgical Center Services," in *March 2020 Report to the Congress: Medicare Payment Policy* (Washington: MedPAC, March 2020).

[22] James C. Robinson, "Comparison Shopping for Knee Surgery," *Wall Street Journal*, October 27, 2013.

[23] James C. Robinson, "Comparison Shopping for Knee Surgery."

[24] Reverse deductibles are akin to vouchers.

[25] James C. Robinson et al., "Association of Reference Payment for Colonoscopy with Consumer Choices, Insurer Spending, and Procedural Complications," *JAMA Internal Medicine* (September 8, 2015); James C. Robinson et al., "Consumer Choice Between Hospital-Based and Freestanding Facilities for Arthroscopy: Impact on Prices, Spending, and Surgical Complications," *Journal of Bone and Joint Surgery* 97, no. 18 (September 16, 2015): 1473–81, https://doi.org/10.2106/jbjs.o.00240; James C. Robinson et al., "Reference-Based Benefit Design Changes Consumers' Choices And Employers' Payments For Ambulatory Surgery," *Health Affairs* 34, no. 3 (March 2015): 415–22, https://doi.org/10.1377/hlthaff.2014.1198 (Adjusted estimate for cataract surgery in this source, which appears in the text, is greater than the unadjusted estimate in the source for Figure 2.2.); and James C. Robinson and Timothy T. Brown, "Increases in Consumer Cost Sharing Redirect Patient Volumes and Reduce Hospital Prices for Orthopedic Surgery," *Health Affairs* 32, no. 8 (2013): 1392–97.

[26] Sherry Glied, *Revising the Tax Treatment of Employer-Provided Health Insurance* (Washington: AEI Press, 1994), p. 19.

[27] Reed Ableson, "UnitedHealth to Insure the Right to Insurance." *New York Times*, December 2, 2008.

[28] John H. Cochrane, "Health-Status Insurance: How Markets Can Provide Health Security," Cato Institute Policy Analysis no. 633, February 18, 2009.

Chapter 3

[1] Institute of Medicine, *Learning What Works: Infrastructure Required for Comparative Effective Research: Workshop Summary* (Washington: The National Academies Press, 2011), p. 97.

[2] Michael F. Cannon and Jacqueline Pohida, "Would 'Medicare for All' Mean Quality for All? How Public-Option Principles Could Reverse Medicare's Negative Impact on Quality," *Quinnipiac Health Law Journal* 25, no. 2 (2022), 198.

[3] Elliot Fisher, "More Care is Not Better Care: Regional Differences Show That Spending More Does Not Improve–and May Hurt–Patients. More Accountability Can Help," National Institute for Health Care Management, *Expert Voices* 7 (January 2005).

[4] Martin A. Makary and Michael Daniel, "Medical Error—The Third Leading Cause of Death in the US," *BMJ* 353 (May 3, 2016), https://doi.org/10.1136/bmj.i2139.

[5] John T. James, "A New, Evidence-based Estimate of Patient Harms Associated with Hospital Care," *Journal of Patient Safety* 9, no. 3 (September 2013): 122–28, http://doi.org/10.1097/PTS.0b013e3182948a69.

[6] Sherry L. Murphy et al., "Mortality in the United States, 2020," National Center for Health Statistics Data Brief no. 427, Centers for Disease Control and Prevention, December 2021.

[7] Jiaquan Xu et al., "Deaths: Final Data for 2019," *National Vital Statistics Reports* 70, no. 8 (July 2021); Andrew P. Wilper et al., "Health Insurance and Mortality in US Adults," *American Journal of Public Health* 99, no. 12 (December 2009), https://doi.org/10.2105/AJPH.2008.157685. "Lack of health insurance is associated with as many as 44,789 deaths per year in the United States," among those aged 18 to 64 in 2005. See also Janice Hopkins Tanne, "26,000 Americans Die Each Year Because of Lack of Insurance, *BMJ* 336 (April 19, 2018): 855.

[8] Irene Papanicolas, Liana R. Woskie, and Ashish K. Jha, "Health Care Spending in the United States and Other High-Income Countries," *JAMA* 319, no. 10 (March 13, 2018): 1024–39, http://doi.org/10.1001/jama.2018.1150.

[9] James C. Robinson, Timothy T. Brown, and Christopher Whaley, "Reference Pricing Changes the 'Choice Architecture' of Health Care for Consumers," *Health Affairs* 36, no. 3 (March 2017): 524–30, https://doi.org/10.1377/hlthaff.2016.1256; Edward H. Wagner, Nirmala Sandhu, Katherine M. Newton et al., "Effect of Improved Glycemic Control on Health Care Costs and Utilization," *JAMA* 285, no. 2 (January 10, 2001):182–89, http://doi.org/10.1001/jama.285.2.182; Clayton M. Christensen, Jerome Grossman, and Jason Hwang, *The Innovator's Prescription: A Disruptive Solution for Health Care* (New York: McGraw-Hill, 2009); and Tara Bannow, "Oregon Nurse Practitioners Can Now Perform Vasectomies," *The Bulletin*, August 1, 2017.

[10] Thankfully, that book already exists. See Charles Silver and David Hyman, *Overcharged: Why Americans Pay Too Much for Health Care* (Washington: Cato Institute, 2018).

[11] See Michael F. Cannon, "Is Obamacare Harming Quality? (Part 1)," *Health Affairs* (blog), January 4, 2018; Michael F. Cannon, "How to Ensure Quality Health Coverage (Part 2)," *Health Affairs* (blog), January 5, 2018; and Michael F. Cannon, "Obamacare Makes Discrimination against Those with Preexisting Conditions Even Worse," *Washington Examiner*, December 7, 2020.

Chapter 4

[1] "How to Pay for Universal Health Care: It is More Attainable in Developing Countries than You May Think," *The Economist* (film), December 1, 2022.

[2] "Health Spending: Government/Compulsory, Percentage of Health Spending, 2020," Organisation for Economic Co-operation and Development (OECD).

[3] Figures and rankings for 2019 are similar. In 2019, Norway ranked 1st (86 percent), the United States ranked 9th (83 percent), the United Kingdom ranked 14th (79 percent) and Canada ranked 28th (70 percent). "Health Spending: Total/Government/Compulsory, Percentage of GDP, 2020" OECD.

[4] See Jeffrey A. Singer and Michael F. Cannon, "Drug Reformation: End Government's Power to Require Prescriptions," Cato Institute White Paper, October 20, 2020.

Chapter 5

[1] Harvard Business School professor Clayton Christensen explains, "Many of the most powerful innovations that disrupted other industries did so by enabling a larger population of less-skilled people to do in a more convenient, less-expensive setting things that historically could be performed only by expensive specialists in centralized, inconvenient locations." Clayton M. Christensen, Richard M. J. Bohmer, and John Kenagy, "Will Disruptive Innovations Cure Health Care?," *Harvard Business Review*, September–October 2000.

[2] Paul Starr, *The Social Transformation of American Medicine* (New York: Basic Books, 1982).

[3] American Medical Association, "AMA Successfully Fights Scope of Practice Expansions That Threaten Patient Safety," Scope of Practice, Chicago, May 15, 2023.

[4] William Allen Pusey, "The Disappearance of Doctors from Small Towns," *Journal of the American Medical Association* 88, no. 7 (February 12, 1927): 505–6.

[5] Clayton M. Christensen, Jerome Grossman, and Jason-Hwang, *The Innovator's Prescription: A Disruptive Solution for Health Care* (New York: McGraw-Hill, 2009).

[6] Darcy Devine, "Valuing Physician-Performed NP & PA Supervisory Services," BuckheadFMV, March 19, 2017. See also "Stipends for Physician Supervision of NPPs Gain Traction, But Some Stark Risk Exists," *Report on Medicare Compliance* 27, no. 16 (April 30, 2018). Estimating a fair-market-value supervision arrangement stipend of $12,000.

[7] Richard Allen, "Physician and Nonphysician Licensure and Scope of Practice," Report of the Council on Medical Education, American Medical Association, CME Report 1-I-00, 2000, p. 250.

[8] Bethany Davidson, "New Tennessee Laws Go Into Effect Today; What You Need To Know," News Channel 5, Nashville, July 1, 2020.

[9] Testimony in favor of AB 228, Assembly Committee on Commerce and Labor, 77th Nevada Legislature (2013), (Stan Brock, Founder and Volunteer Director of Operations, Remote Area Medical).

[10] Associated Press, "Medical Volunteers Not Free To Cross State Lines," *Arkansas Democrat Gazette*, July 21, 2012.

[11] C-Span, "Washington Journal, Health Care and the Underinsured," C-Span video, 31:15, October 17, 2009.

[12] U.S. Bureau of the Census, "Historical Statistics of the United States, Colonial Times to 1970, Bicentennial Edition," Part 1, Chapter B, "Vital Statistics and Health and Medical Care" (Series B 1–220), Washington, 1975.

[13] See Paul Starr, *The Social Transformation of American Medicine: The Rise of a Sovereign Profession and the Making of a Vast Industry* (New York: Basic Books, 1982) p. 124; Reuben A Kessel, "The A.M.A. and the Supply of Physicians," *Law and Contemporary Problems* 35 (Spring 1970): 271.

[14] Kaiser Family Foundation, "Professionally Active Physicians by Gender," KFF, May 2023; "Women in Medicine: A Review of Changing Physician Demographics, Female Physicians by Specialty, State and Related Data," Staff Care, AMN Healthcare, 2015; and Megan Johnson, "The Healthcare Future Is Female," athenahealth, February 14, 2018.

[15] See generally Michael F. Cannon and Jacqueline Pohida, "Would 'Medicare for All' Mean Quality for All? How Public-Option Principles Could Reverse Medicare's Negative Impact on Quality," *Quinnipiac Health Law Journal* 25, no. 2 (April 8, 2022).

[16] Atul A. Gwande et al., "Does Dissatisfaction with Health Plans Stem from Having No Choices?," *Health Affairs* 17, no. 5 (September/October 1998), https://doi.org/10.1377/hlthaff.17.5.184.

[17] Michael A. Morrisey, "History of Health Insurance in the United States," in *Health Insurance*, 2nd ed. (Washington: Health Administration Press, 2013), p. 9.

[18] Kristine Goodwin, "The Evolving State of Occupational Licensing, Research, State Policies and Trends, 2nd Edition," National Conference of State Legislatures, November 2019.

[19] National Conference of State Legislatures, National Governors Association, and the Council of State Governments, *Occupational Licensing: Assessing State Policies and Practices Final Report* (Washington: National Conference of State Legislatures, December 2020), p. 21.

[20] Public Citizen's Congress Watch, *The Great Medical Malpractice Hoax: NPDB Data Continue to Show Medical Liability System Produces Rational Outcomes* (Washington: Public Citizen's Congress Watch, January 2007).

[21] Testimony in favor of AB 228, Assembly Committee on Commerce and Labor.

[22] Testimony in favor of AB 228, Assembly Committee on Commerce and Labor.

Chapter 6

[1] Michael Morrisey, "State Health Care Reform: Protecting the Provider," in *American Health Care: Government, Market Processes, and the Public Interest*, ed. Roger Feldman (New Brunswick, NJ: Transaction, 2000).

[2] Vivian Ho and Meei-Hsiang Ku-Goto, "State Deregulation and Medicare Costs for Acute Cardiac Care," *Medical Care Research and Review* 70, no. 2 (April 2013), https://doi.org/10.1177/1077558712459681.

[3] Daniel Polsky et al., "The Effect of Entry Regularion in the Health Care Sector: The Case of Home Health," *Journal of Public Economics* 110 (February 2014): 1–14, http://doi.org/10.1016/j.jpubeco.20 13.11.003.

[4] Morrisey, "State Health Care Reform."

[5] Sallyanne Payton and Rhoda M. Powsner, "Regulation through the Looking Glass: Hospitals, Blue Cross, and Certificate-of-Need," *Michigan Law Review* 79, no. 2 (December 1980): 203–77, https://doi.org/10.2307/1288275.

Chapter 7

[1] Ernst R. Berndt et al., "Assessing the Impacts of the Prescription Drug User Fee Acts (PDUFA) on the FDA Approval Process," National Bureau of Economic Research Working Paper no. 10822, October 2004.

[2] Henry I. Miller, *To America's Health: A Proposal to Reform the Food and Drug Administration* (California: Hoover Institution Press, August 1, 2000).

[3] Leah Isakov, Andrew W. Lo, and Vahid Montazerhodjat, "Is the FDA Too Conservative or Too Aggressive?: A Bayesian Decision Analysis of Clinical Trial Design," *Journal of Econometrics* 211 (2019).

[4] Mary K. Olson, "Are Novel Drugs More Risky for Patients than Less Novel Drugs?," *Journal of Health Economics* 23, no. 6 (2004).

[5] T. Philipson et al., "Cost-Benefit Analysis of the FDA: The Case of the Prescription Drug User Fee Acts," *Journal of Public Economics* 92, no. 5–6 (June 2008): 1306–25.

[6] Sam Peltzman, "By Prescription Only . . . or Occasionally?," *Regulation* 11, no. 3 (Fall/Winter 1987): 23–28.

[7] Peltzman, "By Prescription Only . . . or Occasionally?"

[8] Sam Peltzman, "The Health Effects of Mandatory Prescriptions," *Journal of Law and Economics* 30, no. 2 (October 1987).

[9] Harry M. Marks, "Revisiting 'The Origins of Compulsory Drug Prescriptions,'" *American Journal of Public Health* 85, no. 1 (January 1995): 109–15.

[10] Peter Temin, "Regulation and the Choice of Prescription Drugs," *American Economic Review* 70, no. 2 (May 1980): 301–5.

[11] Julie Donohue, "A History of Drug Advertising: The Evolving Roles of Consumers and Consumer Protection," *Milbank Quarterly* 84, no. 4 (December 2006): 659–99.

Chapter 8

[1] Bernard Black et al., *Medical Malpractice Litigation: How It Works—Why Tort Reform Hasn't Helped* (Washington: Cato Institute, 2021).

[2] Black et al., *Medical Malpractice Litigation*, p. 89.

[3] Heather Morton, "Medical Liability/Medical Malpractice Laws," National Conference of State Legislatures, July 13, 2021.

[4] Black et al., *Medical Malpractice Litigation*, pp. 116–20.

[5] Black et al., *Medical Malpractice Litigation*, p. 11.

[6] Richard H. Thaler and Cass R. Sunstein, *Nudge: Improving Decisions about Health, Wealth, and Happiness* (New Haven: Yale University Press, 2008).

Chapter 9

[1] Beatriz Duque Long, Carl Schmid, and Andrew Sperling, "Re: 2017 Qualified Health Plan Review and 2018 *Notice of Benefit and Payment Parameters* Rule & Letter to Issuers," letter to the Honorable Sylvia Matthews Burwell, Secretary of Health and Human Services, August 24, 2016.

[2] Michael Geruso, Timothy Layton, and Daniel Prinz, "Screening in Contract Design: Evidence from the ACA Health Insurance Exchanges," *American Economic Journal: Economic Policy* 11, no. 2 (May 2019): 64–107.

[3] Sen. Ron Johnson and Sen. Mike Lee, "Dear Colleague," letter, July 19, 2017, including attachments: "Premium Reconciliation and Pre-ACA Deep Dive," undated; Assistant Secretary for Planning and Evaluation, "Estimating the Effects of the Consumer Freedom Amendment on the Individual Market," U.S. Department of Health and Human Services, July 15, 2017.

[4] Assistant Secretary for Planning and Evaluation, "Individual Market Premium Changes: 2013–2017," U.S. Department of Health and Human Services, May 23, 2017.

[5] "Rate Review," HealthCare.gov, accessed September 1, 2023.

[6] "I asked one of the [authors] of the study, Mark Pauly, why it seems that older women are bearing the brunt. 'It's likely because they are being averaged in with younger women who have much higher expenses associated with childbearing and with older men who didn't take care of themselves. Community rating redistributes against the relatively healthy,' he explained." Joann Weiner, "Older Women Bear the Brunt of Higher Insurance Costs under Obamacare," *Washington Post*, June 24, 2014.

[7] Brian Blase, "Expanded ACA Subsidies: Exacerbating Health Inflation and Income Inequality," Galen Institute, June 2021.

[8] Foundation for Government Accountability, "34-State Poll Confirms Voters Don't Want State-Run Obamacare Exchanges," press release, March 26, 2015.

[9] Michael Geruso, "Screening in Exchanges: Some Facts and Findings from Geruso, Layton, Prinz," Penn LDI HIX Conference, September 2017; Geruso, Layton, and Prinz, "Screening in Contract Design"; and Long, Schmid, and Sperling, "Re: 2017 Qualified Health Plan Review."

[10] Geruso, Layton, and Prinz, "Screening in Contract Design."

[11] Finding half of entries in community-rated plan-provider directories either were not in network or were not accepting patients. Jack S. Resneck Jr. et al., "The Accuracy of Dermatology Network Physician Directories Posted by Medicare Advantage Health Plans in an Era of Narrow Networks," *JAMA Dermatol* 150, no. 12 (December 2014): 1290–7. And nearly half of entries in community-rated plan-provider directories were inaccurate. Centers for Medicare & Medicaid Services, "Online Provider Directory Review Report," January 13, 2017.

[12] Geruso, "Screening in Exchanges."

[13] David M. Culter and Sarah J. Reber, "Paying for Health Insurance: The Trade-Off between Competition and Adverse Selection," *Quarterly Journal of Economics* 113, no. 2 (May 1998): 433–66; and Karen Davis, Barbara S. Cooper, and Rose Capasso, "The Federal Employee Health Benefits Program: A Model for Workers, Not Medicare," The Commonwealth Fund, November 2003.

[14] Geruso, Layton, and Prinz, "Screening in Contract Design"; Avalere, "Health Plans with More Restrictive Provider Networks Continue to Dominate the Exchange Market," press release, December 4, 2018; and Avalere, "Exchange Plans Include 34 Percent Fewer Providers than the Average for Commercial Plans," July 15, 2015.

[15] Geruso, "Screening in Exchanges"; Geruso, Layton, and Prinz, "Screening in Contract Design"; and Long, Schmid, and Sperling, "Re: 2017 Qualified Health Plan Review."

[16] Michael F. Cannon, "BCBSNC's Premium Refunds Show the Perils of ObamaCare," *Charlotte Observer*, October 6, 2010.

[17] Sarah Lueck, "States Should Structure Insurance Exchanges to Minimize Adverse Selection," Center on Budget and Policy Priorities, August 17, 2010; and Brief for America's Health Insurance Plans and the Blue Cross Blue Shield Association as Amici Curiae, *National Federation of Independent Business v. Sebelius, Department of Health & Human Services v. Florida, Florida v. Department of Health and Human Services*, January 6, 2012, Nos. 11-393, 11-398, 11-400.

[18] "Ranking Member Report: Health Care Reform Law's Impact on Child-Only Health Insurance Policies," Senate Committee on Health, Education, Labor and Pensions, 112th Cong., August 2, 2011.

[19] Congressional Budget Office, *Federal Subsidies for Health Insurance Coverage for People Under Age 65: CBO and JCT's May 2023 Baseline Projections* (Washington: Congressional Budget Office, 2023).

[20] Peter Siegelman and Tom Baker, "Tontines for the Invincibles: Enticing Low Risks into the Health Insurance Pool with an Idea from Insurance History and Behavioral Economics," University of Connecticut, Faculty Articles and Papers, 2010.

[21] John H. Cochrane, "Health Status Insurance: How Markets Can Provide Health Security," Cato Institute Policy Analysis no. 633, February 18, 2009.

[22] Mark Pauly, "How Private Health Insurance Pools Risk," *NBER Reporter*, September 2005.

[23] Ashley Noble, "Any Willing or Authorized Provider," National Conference of State Legislatures, November 5, 2014.

[24] Michael Morrisey, "State Health Care Reform: Protecting the Provider," in American Health Care: Government, Market Processes, and the Public Interest, ed. Roger Feldman (New Brunswick, NJ: Transaction, 2000), p. 252.

[25] Victoria C. Bunce, "Health Insurance Mandates in the States 2012: Executive Summary," The Council for Affordable Health Insurance, 2013.

[26] Miriam J. Laugesen et al., "A Comparative Analysis of Mandated Benefit Laws, 1949-2002," *Health Services Research* 41, no. 3 (June 2006, Pt. 2): 1081–1103, http://doi.org/10.1111/j.1475-6773.2006.00521.x; and Cindy Farquhar et al., "High-Dose Chemotherapy and Autologous Bone Marrow or Stem Cell Transplantation Versus Conventional Chemotherapy for Women With Early Poor Prognosis Breast Cancer," *Cochrane Database of Systematic Reviews* 5 (May 20, 2016), https://doi.org/10.1002/14651858.CD003139.pub3.

[27] Congressional Budget Office, *Increasing Small-Firm Health Insurance Coverage Through Association Health Plans and Healthmarts* (Washington: Congressional Budget Office, January 2000).

[28] Michael F. Cannon, "Short-Term Plans Would Increase Coverage, Protect Conscience Rights & Improve Obamacare Risk Pools," *Cato at Liberty* (blog), Cato Institute, July 2, 2018.

[29] Michael F. Cannon, "Re: Comments on Short-Term, Limited Duration Insurance—CMS-9924-P," letter to Seema Verma, Centers for Medicare & Medicaid Services, April 23, 2018.

[30] Cannon, "Re: Comments on Short-Term, Limited Duration Insurance—CMS-9924-P."

[31] Chris Pope, *Renewable Term Health Insurance: Better Coverage than Obamacare* (New York: Manhattan Institute, May 2019).

[32] Michael F. Cannon, Cato Institute, "Regarding SB 199—Short-Term Limited Duration Plans," Testimony before the Kansas Senate Committee on Financial Institutions and Insurance, March 25, 2021.

[33] Marilyn Tavenner, Centers for Medicare and Medicaid Services, letter to Commissioner Gregory R. Francis, Office of Lieutenant Governor, Virgin Islands, July 16, 2014.

[34] Michael F. Cannon, "Give Floridians Additional Choices Alongside Obamacare," *South Florida Sun Sentinel*, May 16, 2022.

[35] Vanessa C. Forsberg and Ryan J. Rosso, "Applicability of Federal Requirements to Selected Health Coverage Arrangements: An Overview," In Focus, Congressional Research Service, November 13, 2019.

[36] Henry N. Butler and Larry E. Ribstein, "The Single-License Solution," *Regulation* 31, no. 4 (Winter 2008–09): 36–42.

[37] Leslie Wayne, "How Delaware Thrives as a Corporate Tax Haven," *New York Times*, June 30, 2012.

Chapter 10

[1] Gary Claxton et al., *Employer Health Benefits: 2021 Annual Survey* (San Francisco, Kaiser Family Foundation, 2021), p. 65.

[2] Bureau of Labor Statistics, "Number of Jobs, Labor Market Experience, and Earnings Growth: Results from a National Longitudinal Survey," Economic News Release, last modified August 31, 2021; and Bureau of Labor Statistics, "Employee Benefits in the United States, March 2020."

[3] Sherry Glied, *Revising the Tax Treatment of Employer Provided Health Insurance* (Washington: AEI Press, 1994).

[4] Carolanne H. Hoffmann, "Health Insurance Coverage, United States: July 1962–June 1963," *Vital Health Stat.* 10, no. 11 (August 1964): 1–37.

[5] Martin Feldstein and Bernard Friedman, "Tax Subsidies, the Rational Demand For Insurance and the Health Care Crisis," *Journal of Public Economics* 7, no. 2 (April 1977): 155–78.

[6] Michael F. Cannon, Cato Institute, Antitrust Applied: Hospital Consolidation Concerns and Solutions, Testimony before the Subcommittee on Competition Policy, Antitrust, and Consumer Rights, Committee on the Judiciary, 117th Congress, May 19, 2021.

Chapter 11

[1] John A. Poisal et al., "National Health Expenditure Projections, 2021–30: Growth to Moderate As COVID-19 Impacts Wane," *Health Affairs* 41, no. 4 (March 28, 2022), https://doi.org/10.1377/hlthaff.2022.00113.

[2] Michael F. Cannon and Jacqueline Pohida, "Would 'Medicare for All' Mean Quality for All? How Public-Option Principles Could Reverse Medicare's Negative Impact on Quality," *Quinnipiac Health Law Journal* 25, no. 2 (April 8, 2022): 183n2.

[3] Sherry Glied, *Revising the Tax Treatment of Employer–Provided Health Insurance* (Washington: AEI Press, 1994), pp. 19, 35n76.

[4] Sherry Glied, *Revising the Tax Treatment of Employer–Provided Health Insurance.*

[5] Michael F. Cannon, "End the Tax Exclusion for Employer-Sponsored Health Insurance: Return $1 Trillion to the Workers Who Earned It," Cato Institute Policy Analysis no. 928 (May 24, 2022).

[6] Carolanne H. Hoffmann, "Health Insurance Coverage, United States: July 1962–June 1963," *Vital Health Stat.* 10, no. 11 (August 1964): 1–37.

[7] Dartmouth Atlas Project, *The Dartmouth Atlas of Health Care* (website).

[8] Cannon and Pohida, "Would 'Medicare for All' Mean Quality for All?"

[9] MedPAC, "Chapter 7: Using Incentives to Improve the Quality of Care in Medicare," in *June 2003 Report to the Congress: Variation and Innovation* (Washington: MedPAC, June 12, 2003), p. 108.

[10] Thomas C. Tsai et al., "Better Patient Care at High-Quality Hospitals May Save Medicare Money and Bolster Episode-Based Payment Models," *Health Affairs* 35, no. 9 (September 2016): 1681, https://doi.org/10.1377/hlthaff.2016.0361.

[11] Amy Finkelstein and Robin McKnight, "What Did Medicare Do? The Initial Impact of Medicare on Mortality and Out of Pocket Medical Spending," *Journal of Public Economics* 92, no. 7 (July 2008): 1644, https://doi.org/10.1016/j.jpubeco.2007.10.005.

[12] U.S. Office of Management and Budget, "Table 3.2—Outlays by Function and Subfunction: 1962–2028," FY 2024 President's Budget Historical Tables; U.S. Office of Management and Budget, "Table 10.1—Gross Domestic Product and Deflators Used in the Historical Tables: 1940–2027," FY 2024 President's Budget Historical Tables; and author's calculations.

[13] The Boards of Trustees, Federal Hospital Insurance, and Federal Supplementary Medical Insurance Trust Funds, "The 2021 Annual Report of the Boards of Trustees of the Federal Hospital Insurance and Federal Supplementary Medical Insurance Trust Funds," letter of transmittal, August 31, 2021.

[14] MedPAC, "Chapter 5: Ambulatory Surgical Center Services," in *March 2020 Report to the Congress: Medicare Payment Policy* (Washington: MedPAC, March 2020).

[15] U.S. Department of Health and Human Services, Office of the Assistant Secretary for Planning and Evaluation (ASPE), "Comparison of U.S. and International Prices for Top Medicare Part B Drugs by Total Expenditures," October 25, 2018.

[16] U.S. Department of Health and Human Services, Office of Inspector General, *Medicare and Beneficiaries Paid Substantially More to Provider-Based Facilities in Eight Selected States in Calendar Years 2010 through 2017 Than They Paid to Freestanding Facilities in the Same States for the Same Type of Services* (Washington: DHHS, June 2022).

[17] Amitabh Chandra and Craig Garthwaite, "Economic Principles for Medicare Reform," *The ANNALS of the American Academy of Political and Social Science* 686, no. 1 (November 6, 2019), https://doi.org/10.1177/0002716219885582; Jeffrey Clemens and Joshua D. Gottlieb, "In the Shadow of a Giant: Medicare's Influence on Private Physician Payments," *Journal of Political Economy* 125, no. 1 (February 2017), https://doi.org/10.1086/689772.

[18] Martin S. Feldstein, "The Rising Price of Physicians' Services," *Review of Economics and Statistics* 52, no. 2, (May 1970): 121–33; and Martin S. Feldstein, *The Rising Cost of Hospital Care*, National Center for Health Services Research and Development (Washington: Information Resources Press, 1971).

[19] Amy Finkelstein, "The Aggregate Effects of Health Insurance: Evidence from the Introduction of Medicare," *Quarterly Journal of Economics* 122, no. 1 (February 2007), p. 24, 32.

[20] Finkelstein, "The Aggregate Effects of Health Insurance," p. 22.

[21] See generally U.S. Congressional Budget Office, "Lessons from Medicare's Demonstration Projects on Disease Management, Care Coordination, and Value-Based Payment," Issue Brief, January 2012; and Cannon and Pohida, "Would 'Medicare for All' Mean Quality for All?"

[22] Mark V. Pauly, *Markets without Magic: How Competition Might Save Medicare* (Washington: AEI Press, 2018), p. 12.

[23] Jonathan D. Ketcham et al., "Sinking, Swimming, or Learning to Swim in Medicare Part D," *American Economic Review* 102, no. 6 (October 2012): 2639–73, http://doi.org/10.1257/aer.102.6.2639.

Chapter 12

[1] Centers for Medicare & Medicaid Services, "Annual Medicaid & CHIP Expenditures," Medicaid.gov.

[2] John A. Poisal et al., "National Health Expenditure Projections, 2021–30: Growth to Moderate as COVID-19 Impacts Wane," *Health Affairs* 41, no. 4 (March 28, 2022), https://www.healthaffairs.org/doi/epdf/10.1377/hlthaff.2022.00113.

[3] John A. Poisal et al., "National Health Expenditure Projections, 2021–30."

[4] "Strengthening Medicaid Program Integrity," Current High Risk List, Government Accountability Office.

[5] Mark Duggan and Fiona M. Scott Morton, "The Distortionary Effects of Government Procurement: Evidence from Medicaid Prescription Drug Purchasing," *Quarterly Journal of Economics* 121, no. 1 (February 2006): 1–30, https://doi.org/10.1093/qje/121.1.1.

[6] "Medicaid and CHIP Income Eligibility Limits for Children as a Percent of the Federal Poverty Level," Kaiser Family Foundation, n.d.

[7] Katherine Baicker et al., "The Oregon Experiment—Effects of Medicaid on Clinical Outcomes," *New England Journal of Medicine* 368 (May 2, 2013): 1713–22.

[8] Steven D. Pizer, Austin Frakt, and Lisa Iezzoni, "The Effect of Health Reform on Public and Private Insurance in the Long Run," U.S. Department of Veterans Affairs, Boston University School of Public Health, and Harvard Medical School, March 9, 2011. For subsequent research on crowd-out by Obamacare's Medicaid expansion, see Stephen R. Barnes et al., "Preliminary Assessment of Crowd Out in Louisiana: Insights From the Louisiana Health Insurance Survey," E. J. Ourso College of Business, LSU, March 12, 2019.

[9] Hayden Dublois and Jonathan Ingram, "An Unsustainable Path: How ObamaCare's Medicaid Expansion Is Causing an Enrollment and Budget Crisis," Foundation for Government Accountability, January 2022.

[10] Congressional Budget Office, *Federal Subsidies for Health Insurance Coverage for People Under Age 65: CBO and JCT's May 2023 Baseline Projections* (Washington: Congressionnal Budget Office, May 2023), p. 3.

Chapter 13

[1] U.S. Office of Management and Budget, "Table 3.2—Outlays by Function and Subfunction: 1962–2028," FY 2024 President's Budget Historical Tables.

[2] Linda J. Bilmes, "The Long-Term Costs of United States Care for Veterans of the Afghanistan and Iraq Wars," Watson Institute for International and Public Affairs, Brown University, August 18, 2021.

[3] U.S. Department of Veterans Affairs, *FY 2024 Budget Submission: Budget in Brief* (Washington: U.S. Department of Veterans Affairs, March 2023).

[4] U.S. Department of Veterans Affairs, *FY 2024 Budget Submission*, pp. 1, 16.

[5] Paul G. Shekelle et al., "Comparison of Quality of Care in VA and Non-VA Settings: A Systematic Review," Department of Veterans Affairs, Health Services Research & Development Service, September 2010.

[6] Sudhakar V. Nuti et al., "Association of Admission to Veterans Affairs Hospitals vs Non-Veterans Affairs Hospitals With Mortality and Readmission Rates Among Older Men Hospitalized With Acute Myocardial Infarction, Heart Failure, or Pneumonia," *JAMA* 315, no. 6 (February 9, 2016): 582–92, https://doi.org/10.1001/jama.2016.0278.

[7] U.S. Congressional Budget Office, *Options for Reducing the Deficit: 2019 to 2028* (Washington: CBO, December 13, 2018), pp. 107–14, 186–7.

[8] Quil Lawrence, "VA Health Care's Chronic Ailments: Long Waits and Red Tape," NPR, June 4, 2014.

[9] Eyder Peralta, "Audit Finds 13 Percent Of VA Schedulers Told to Falsify Data," NPR, June 9, 2014.

[10] Quil Lawrence, Eric Whitney, and Michael Tomsic, "Despite $10B 'Fix,' Veterans Are Waiting Even Longer to See Doctors," NPR, May 16, 2016.

[11] U.S. Department of Veterans Affairs, "Pending Appointment and Electronic Wait List Summary – National, Facility, and Division Level Summaries Wait Time Calculated from Preferred Date," March 15, 2021, p. 34.

[12] Leo Shane III, "Veterans Disability Claims Backlog Expected to Grow in Coming Months," *Military Times*, September 16, 2021.

[13] Debra A. Draper, director, Health Care of the U.S. Government Accountability Office, Veterans Health Care: Opportunities Remain to Improve Appointment Scheduling within VA and through Community Care, Testimony before the Committee on Veterans' Affairs, 116th Cong. (2019).

[14] Draper, testimony.

[15] Matthew S. Goldberg, deputy assistant director, National Security Division of the Congressional Budget Office, Comparing the Costs of the Veterans' Health Care System With Private-Sector Costs, Testimony before the Subcommittee on Health Committee on Veterans' Affairs, 144th Cong. (2015).

[16] U.S. Department of Veterans Affairs, *Fiscal Year 2022 Agency Financial Report* (Washington: Department of Veterans Affairs, 2022), p. 21; and Congressional Budget Office, *The Budget and Economic Outlook: 2023 to 2033* (Washington: CBO, 2023), p.6; and author's calculations.

[17] Hearing on the True Cost of the War, Before the Committee on Veterans' Affairs, 111th Cong., 2nd sess., (September 30, 2010), p. 40 (statement of Linda J. Bilmes, Daniel Patrick Moynihan Senior Lecturer in Public Policy, John F. Kennedy School of Government, Harvard University, and Joseph E. Stiglitz, professor, Columbia University).

[18] U.S. Department of Veterans Affairs, *Fiscal Year 2022 Agency Financial Report*, p. 29.

[19] U.S. Department of Veterans Affairs, *Fiscal Year 2022 Agency Financial Report*, p. 21.

[20] U.S. Department of Veterans Affairs, *Fiscal Year 2022 Agency Financial Report*, p. 21.

Chapter 14

[1] Milton Friedman, *Capitalism and Freedom* (Chicago: University of Chicago Press, 1962).

[2] Shirley V. Svorny and Michael F. Cannon, "Health Care Workforce Reform: COVID-19 Spotlights Need for Changes to Clinician Licensing," Cato Institute Policy Analysis no. 899, August 4, 2020.

About the Author

Michael F. Cannon is the Cato Institute's director of health policy studies. Cannon is "an influential health-care wonk" (*Washington Post*), "ObamaCare's single most relentless antagonist" (*New Republic*), "ObamaCare's fiercest critic" (*The Week*), "the intellectual father" of *King v. Burwell* (*Modern Healthcare*), and "the most famous libertarian health care scholar" (*Washington Examiner*). *Washingtonian* magazine named Cannon one of Washington, D.C.'s "Most Influential People" in 2021, 2022, and 2023.

Cannon is the coeditor of *Replacing Obamacare: The Cato Institute on Health Care Reform*, author of *50 Vetoes: How States Can Stop the Obama Health Care Law*, and coauthor of *Healthy Competition: What's Holding Back Health Care and How to Free It*. Previously, he served as a domestic policy analyst for the U.S. Senate Republican Policy Committee, where he advised the Senate leadership on health, education, labor, welfare, and the Second Amendment.

Cannon holds an MA in economics and a JM in law and economics from George Mason University and a BA in American government from the University of Virginia. He is a member of the Board of Advisers of *Harvard Health Policy Review* and the Federalist Society Regulatory Transparency Project's FDA & Health Working Group.

About the Cato Institute

Founded in 1977, the Cato Institute is a public policy research foundation dedicated to broadening the parameters of policy debate to allow consideration of more options that are consistent with the principles of limited government, individual liberty, and peace. To that end, the Institute strives to achieve greater involvement of the intelligent, concerned lay public in questions of policy and the proper role of government.

The Institute is named for *Cato's Letters*, libertarian pamphlets that were widely read in the American Colonies in the early 18th century and played a major role in laying the philosophical foundation for the American Revolution.

Despite the achievement of the nation's Founders, today virtually no aspect of life is free from government encroachment. A pervasive intolerance for individual rights is shown by government's arbitrary intrusions into private economic transactions and its disregard for civil liberties. And while freedom around the globe has notably increased in the past several decades, many countries have moved in the opposite direction, and most governments still do not respect or safeguard the wide range of civil and economic liberties.

To address those issues, the Cato Institute undertakes an extensive publications program on the complete spectrum of policy issues. Books, monographs, and shorter studies are commissioned to examine the federal budget, Social Security, regulation, military spending, international trade, and myriad other issues.

In order to maintain its independence, the Cato Institute accepts no government funding. Contributions are received from foundations, corporations, and individuals, and other revenue is generated from the sale of publications. The Institute is a nonprofit, tax-exempt, educational foundation under Section 501(c)3 of the Internal Revenue Code.

CATO INSTITUTE
1000 Massachusetts Ave. NW
Washington, DC 20001
www.cato.org